KV-192-580

STUDIES IN FRENCH LITERATURE No. 31

MONTESQUIEU:
LETTRES PERSANES

by

MARK H. WADDICOR

Lecturer in French, University of Exeter

EDWARD ARNOLD

© MARK H. WADDICOR 1977

First published 1977 by
Edward Arnold (Publishers) Ltd
25 Hill Street, London W1X 8LL

Cloth ISBN: 0 7131 5978 2
Paper ISBN: 0 7131 5979 0

Printed in Great Britain by
The Camelot Press Ltd, Southampton

Contents

I gratefully acknowledge the assistance given to me, by my colleague Dr N. Perry, and by my wife, regarding the form of this study.

1. Introduction

Montesquieu's *Lettres persanes* have been popular ever since they first appeared in 1721. The work makes an immediate impact because of its exotic and erotic atmosphere, its wit and exuberance, and its provocative intellectual outlook; but its form and content are disconcerting. It purports to be a series of real letters, mainly written by or addressed to two Persians, Usbek and Rica, who are on a visit to Europe. Usbek, the older of the two men, leaves behind the wives in his harem: Rica, younger and more adaptable, has no such ties. The book begins as a travelogue, with the two men writing to their friends about their journey west. When they reach Paris (in the last years of the reign of Louis XIV), the narrative thread becomes more tenuous, the story being largely superseded by a satirical account of the institutions, manners and beliefs of the French, and of certain important current events. Behind the satire, we frequently discern a more serious and reflective trend; this trend gradually predominates (without, however, completely eclipsing the satire), and we are presented with discussions of philosophical, religious, and political matters, sometimes occupying a series of letters. In the last sixteen letters, we leave the satire and the philosophy, and are plunged into a dramatic dénouement in the grand style: the increasing disorder in the harem (of which there had been ominous hints earlier on), provokes violent reactions on the part of Usbek, who commands his chief eunuch to punish the guilty wives with the utmost severity; when he learns that his orders have been ineffective, he is plunged into despair; finally, his favourite wife announces that she has taken a lover, and dies proclaiming her joy at being free of Usbek's tyranny.

If we are left disconcerted by the *Lettres persanes*, this is partly because it is difficult to decide what sort of work it is: is it primarily a novel, masquerading as a series of letters; is it mainly a satire of France; or is it predominantly a work of philosophical reflection? It is the first aim of this study to answer these questions by an examination of the fictional elements in the *Lettres persanes*, and of their relation to the philosophy.

The other major difficulty of the work lies in the philosophical content itself: if it has unity, this is hidden beneath a fragmented surface, since the ideas are conveyed through more than one character and in a variety of styles. It is the second aim of this study to reveal a consistent philosophy on the part of the author of the *Lettres persanes*, without ignoring the book's real or apparent contradictions, and without resorting to interpretations based on Montesquieu's later works.

Acknowledgements

The publishers' thanks are due to Editions Garnier Frères, Paris, for permission to reproduce copyright material from Montesquieu's *Lettres persanes*, edited by P. Vernière (Classiques Garnier, 1960).

2. *The* Lettres persanes *as a Work of Fiction*

(i) Fictional and philosophical elements

When we consider the form of the *Lettres persanes*, it becomes obvious that they will not fit neatly into a simple category. The work as a whole bears too much evidence of art for the letters to be genuine: the story is a fiction. But are the *Lettres persanes* best described as a work of fiction, that is, a work where recognizable characters are involved in a series of events which lead up to a climax? Or are they to be seen rather as a work of philosophical reflection—taking the word 'philosophy' in the double sense which it often had in the eighteenth century, that is, first, a set of beliefs about man's relation as an individual to the physical and social world in which he lives, and secondly, beliefs about the institutions (mainly religious and political) which shape man's life?

Both descriptions could be apt, since the philosophy and the fiction can be seen as interrelated: the philosophy serves a fictional purpose, in that the views expressed by Usbek and Rica tell us about their characters; the fiction serves a philosophical purpose, in that the story has certain moral and political implications. The work is perhaps best characterized by the hybrid term 'philosophical novel'—a genre which was to become more and more popular as the century progressed. This dual aspect of the work is underlined by Montesquieu in the preface, entitled 'Quelques réflexions sur les *Lettres persanes*', which he wrote some thirty years after the book itself, and in which he abandoned the pretence he had made in the original 'Introduction', that the letters are genuine.[1] Speaking about himself in the third person, he said:

> L'auteur s'est donné l'avantage de pouvoir joindre de la philosophie, de la politique et de la morale, à un roman.[2]

[1] The 'Introduction' is usually printed immediately before the first letter of the *Lettres persanes*. The claim about the genuineness of the letters is made in paragraphs 4–9.

[2] The 'Quelques réflexions sur les *Lettres Persanes*' (which will be referred to as the 'Réflexions') are usually printed immediately before the 'Introduction'. The quotation comes from paragraph 3.

But which of these two aspects, the philosophical or the fictional, was uppermost in his mind? The words just quoted imply that the novel is the basic element, to which the philosophy is appended (this interpretation ties in with Montesquieu's assessment of the reasons for the success of the work: 'Rien n'a plu d'avantage, dans les *Lettres persanes*, que d'y trouver, sans y penser, une espèce de roman' ('Réflexions')). However, it is wise to treat with caution the affirmations made by authors about their intentions in writing a book. This is especially the case with eighteenth-century authors; in that era, and particularly in the middle years of the century, it was dangerous to express religious and political ideas of a critical kind, and authors often tried to hide their real aims by writing defensive prefaces to their works. Now, the 'Réflexions' are partly a reply to a certain abbé Gaultier who, in 1751, had published a pamphlet in which he claimed that the *Lettres persanes* were subversive, particularly in their religious content. By stressing, in the 'Réflexions', the fictional element in the book, and by arguing that the ideas expressed by the Persians are significant purely as a reflection of their psychological development, Montesquieu cleverly defends himself against Gaultier's accusations: he implies that the abbé was mistaken in thinking he was reading a work of philosophy.

So, in order to decide which element, the fictional or the philosophical, is predominant, it is perhaps better to leave the 'Réflexions' aside, and to look at the work itself. We notice that it begins and ends as a novel, but that the fictional element is relatively unimportant (though by no means forgotten), in the letters numbered XXVII–CXLVI:[3] thus the novel occupies the most prominent positions, but the philosophy (together with the social satire) forms the bulk of the content. It seems likely therefore that Montesquieu's fundamental aim was to express certain ideas about life and about society, but that at the same time he wished to do so in an original form, one which would be both challenging to the author and stimulating to the reader.

---

[3] In the present study, the individual letters of the *Lettres persanes* are referred to by capital roman numerals. Readers will thus be able to locate a quotation whatever edition they are using, provided it is based, as most modern ones are, on the 1758 text, which has a total of 161 letters. Particular paragraphs within a letter are indicated by the sign §. All quotations from the *Lettres persanes* are taken from the Garnier edition (Paris, 1960).

(ii) The letter form

The novel in letter form, which was to enjoy great popularity later in the eighteenth century (the novels of Richardson, in England, and in France, *La Nouvelle Héloïse* by Jean-Jaques Rousseau and *Les Liaisons dangereuses* by Laclos, being the best-known examples), was in its infancy at the time Montesquieu was writing, and he was one of the first authors to use letters supposedly written by a number of different correspondents as the sole means of narration. He himself was aware of his originality: 'Mes *Lettres persanes* apprirent à faire des romans en lettres', he proudly stated in his private notebooks, and the 'Réflexions' show that he was very much alive to the consequences of adopting this particular form.

The question of the letter form has to be considered from two angles. First, how does it relate to the philosophical content of the work? Secondly, how does it relate to the fictional element?

Assuming that Montesquieu had a fairly coherent and unified series of ideas to put across, why did he choose the letter form rather than, say, the philosophical discourse, as Descartes had done, or the philosophical dialogue? The dialogue has the disadvantage that it restricts a discussion to a particular occasion, and cannot easily present the evolution of ideas in a character's mind, which is something that Montesquieu wished to do. In any case, the form had already been brought to perfection by Fontenelle, and Montesquieu perhaps did not wish to compete with such a master. His reason for not choosing the discourse could be that it involves a systematization of the author's thoughts which, excellent as that may be for the development of his intellect, tends to make excessive demands on the intelligence and powers of concentration of the reader, and, worse than that, may irritate him by glossing over difficulties or complexities in the name of consistency.

By using the letter form, Montesquieu avoided both of these drawbacks. His thought is not presented rigidly and systematically, but is given either by implication, through a piece of satire (e.g. XXXVII), or allegorically, as in the story of the Troglodytes (XI–XIV), or—and this is the most frequent method—through a letter in the form of a short essay on a particular topic. Good examples of this technique are to be found in certain letters written by Usbek: XLVI and LXXXV on religion, LXIX on the idea of God, LXXX on the best government, LXXXIII on morality, and XCIV–XCV on international justice. The views expressed in these letters are rarely put dogmatically; the fact that Usbek is writing to people he knows and respects precludes such a manner of expression. (The series of letters on the population of the world (CXIII–CXXII) is something of an exception in this respect.) Often the ideas are put forward quite tentatively, as in Letter XVII, where Usbek is exploring the question of why certain things appear to us to be pure or impure. Sometimes we are given more than one point of view of a problem, as in Letters LXXVI–LXXVII on suicide, and Letters CV–CVI on luxury and material progress. It is not always easy to determine the exact point of view of the writer—as in Letter CIV on the English constitution. In general, the reader is not lectured to, but invited to reflect.

The apparent disadvantage of the letter form, as far as the expression of ideas is concerned, is that the book may give an impression of incoherence. Letters on philosophical topics are interspersed with ones which have little to do with ideas, and, if we simply extract the philosophical letters, they do not seem to follow any obvious order. However, a careful reading of the *Lettres persanes* does reveal a kind of pattern, in that letters concerning particular topics tend to occur predominantly in certain parts of the work. Paul Vernière has produced a tabulated analysis of the letters, which shows clearly that those concerned with social satire (including those about nations other than France and Persia) occur at intervals throughout the work, but that they are mostly to be found in the first hundred letters; that the letters on philosophical subjects occur mainly in the middle of the work; that those specifically on religious practices, beliefs and institutions come mainly in the first half, and those on political science mainly in the second half.[4] This obviously represents some kind of structure, but not a rigid one. On the fictional level, it corresponds to the greater understanding of Western society which Usbek gradually acquires; on the intellectual level, it corresponds to a progress from the particular to the general; and on the stylistic level, it corresponds to the gradual adoption of a more serious tone, and to a gradual predominance of letters from Usbek over letters from Rica, at least until the section CXXV–CXLIII.

Thus, by using the letter form, and by carefully selecting the tone and content of each letter, as well as its position within the whole, Montesquieu is able to combine an undogmatic approach with an overall plan which nevertheless remains fairly flexible. A second advantage of

[4] P. xv in the Introduction to the Garnier edition of the *Lettres persanes* (see 'Suggestions for Further Reading', p. 63).

the letter form, as Montesquieu has used it, is the possibility it allows of distancing the writers of the letters from the society they are observing, since they are supposedly natives of a foreign country, and since most of their letters are addressed to other foreigners. The reader is thus invited, in a subtle way, to view himself and his world from the outside. The introduction of a falsely naïve spectator is of course a stock satirical device, and one which was particularly favoured by eighteenth-century writers: some of Voltaire's *contes philosophiques* provide outstanding examples of the technique. What makes Montesquieu's use of the foreign observer particularly interesting is that he avoids the over-simplification often associated with the device, by making his observers characters in their own right.

This brings us to the third advantage of using the letter form to express ideas: directness. Although the characters start by seeming distant, because of their situation and their cultural background, we soon come to know and respect them as people, since we see how they think and feel as we read their letters; this, in turn, tends to confer a kind of validity on the ideas they express.

The quality of directness is also the main advantage achieved by using the letter form for the narration of the story. The supposed authenticity of the letters enables the reader to feel he is in contact with the mind of the person to whom they are attributed; such directness is in some ways more difficult to achieve in a third-person narrative. Montesquieu himself was well aware of this advantage, when he said in the 'Réflexions' that novels in letter form

> réussissent ordinairement, parce que l'on rend compte soi-même de sa situation actuelle; ce qui fait plus sentir les passions que tous les récits qu'on en pourrait faire. (§ 2)

This advantage was perhaps even greater in the early eighteenth century, when some readers were apparently rather gullible, and tended to accept on trust statements, in the prefaces of many memoir-novels and letter-novels, that the manuscripts or letters on which they were based were genuine. But the advantage remains even if we do not accept with our critical mind that the *Lettres persanes* consist of real letters. Our imagination tends to be deceived by this use of the first person, at least until we close the book.

The kind of directness which can result from the letter-novel, provided of course that it is skilfully handled, may also be produced by a first-person narrative, but this form would not have been suitable for Montesquieu's purpose of conveying a variety of temperaments and points of view: its perspective is too narrow. The letter form is also, in a way, analogous to the theatre, for there too the author does not intervene directly, but allows a number of characters to speak for themselves. However, the theatre, while it might have been suitable for the story of the revolution in Usbek's harem (Racine, after all, had written a tragedy, *Bajazet*, on an oriental subject), would not have been suitable, at least in the somewhat rarefied form acceptable to eighteenth-century audiences, for the expression of the wide-ranging ideas that Montesquieu wished to convey. By using the letter form, he is able to combine the directness of the theatre with the diversity of subject-matter and tone possible within the novel.

One obvious disadvantage of the letter form, as regards the narrative, is that it can be a very complicated affair for the author to ensure that the chronology of the sending and receipt of the letters does not interfere with the story-telling, or vice versa. Later in the century, Rousseau attempted to get over this problem by making only the vaguest references, in his letter-novel, to the date when each letter is supposed to be sent or received, while Laclos, in *Les Liaisons dangereuses*, went to the opposite extreme, and constructed a very coherent chronological sequence of letters. Montesquieu's approach is closer to that subsequently to be adopted by Laclos. Every letter is dated according to a system which looks complicated but which, as Robert Shackleton has shown,[5] is really quite simple, and enables Montesquieu to combine exotic vocabulary with European chronology. Montesquieu gives the year, and the day of the month, according to our calendar; he takes the names of the months from the Moslem religious calendar, but instead of making them correspond to the chronology of that calendar, which is based on lunar months, he makes them correspond to the calendar months of our system. Thus

Zilcadé	= January	Gemmadi I	= July
Zilhagé	= February	Gemmadi II	= August
Maharram	= March	Rhegeb	= September
Saphar	= April	Chahban	= October
Rebiab I	= May	Rhamazan	= November
Rebiab II	= June	Chalval	= December

[5] 'The Moslem chronology of the *Lettres persanes*' (see 'Suggestions for Further Reading').

Using this table, we can see that Montesquieu generally respects historical chronology: for example, Letter XCII, which announces the death of Louis XIV, is dated 'le 4 de la lune de Rhegeb, 1715', that is, 4 September 1715, four days after the momentous event occurred. (Sometimes, however, he makes a mistake: Letter XXIV, dated 'le 4 de la lune de Rebiab II, 1712' (4 June 1712) refers to an important Papal Bull which was in fact issued over a year later.)

Montesquieu also respects the chronology of the harem story, at least as far as is necessary to satisfy most readers. In order to do this he paradoxically has to depart from a strictly chronological sequence of letters (that is, a sequence in which letters are printed in the order in which they were written). This is because it takes up to six months for letters to travel between France and Persia (CLV). If Montesquieu had adopted a strictly chronological order, the result would have been that several letters on extraneous topics would have intervened between, say, a letter sent from Persia, and Usbek's reply to it, and the reader might thus lose track of the narrative. Instead, Montesquieu presents the letters in the order in which the two main characters wrote or received them. Thus, for example, Letter LXX (9 July 1714), from Usbek's wife Zélis, is placed immediately before Usbek's reply to it (LXXI, 5 December); in other words, it is placed at about the time Usbek received it; if it had been placed at the time it was written, it would have come between Letters LXIII (10 May) and LXVI (8 October).

There are some exceptions to this convenient scheme, but they are relatively unimportant, except at the end of the work (Letters CXLVII–CLXI), where Montesquieu departs even further from a strictly chronological presentation, so as to eliminate completely the relaxation of tension that would have resulted if the reader had had to read through letters irrelevant to the climax of the harem story, in order to reach those directly concerned with it. If he had followed the previously-established scheme, Montesquieu would have placed Letter CXLVII, announcing the disorders in the harem and dated 1 September 1717, between Usbek's two letters of 4 October 1717 (CXI) and 8 October 1718 (CXIII), since it reached him in February 1718; similarly, Letters CXLVIII–CLVIII would all have found their place, according to the scheme, in the series CXI–CXLVI, though letters CLIX–CLXI, which presumably reached Usbek at about the time he wrote his last philosophical letter (CXLVI), would still have come last. Instead, Montesquieu places together all the letters concerning the disintegration of the harem, thus ensuring unity of action at the conclusion of the work.

This departure from the usual pattern has additional advantages. During the first hundred letters, Montesquieu has been careful to remind us, at fairly regular intervals, of the existence of the harem and of the fact that it still preoccupies Usbek after his arrival in France (Letters XXVI, XLI–XLIII, XLVII, LIII, LXII, LXIV–LXV, LXX–LXXI, LXXIX, XCVI); but between Letters XCVI and CXLVII, we lose sight of it almost completely. Montesquieu thus lulls us into thinking that all is quiet there, and makes the final catastrophe more unexpected. Moreover, when we eventually read Letter CXLVII, and realize that Usbek had known since 1717 that trouble was brewing, we conclude that his intense philosophizing in the years 1717–20 was an attempt on his part to forget about what deeply concerned him. By his skilful manipulation of chronology, Montesquieu achieves at the same time dramatic tension and psychological plausibility.

The climax of the story is carefully arranged so as to achieve the maximum of effect with the minimum of material: it is all over in sixteen brief letters, each of which marks a significant development in the plot. The troubles in the harem are announced (CXLVII); Usbek orders severe punishments (CXLVIII); the chief eunuch dies before these orders arrive, and his successor is an incompetent idiot who is unaware of what is happening and who does not dare to open Usbek's letter (CXLIX); Usbek has to write again with renewed orders of severity (CL), but this letter is intercepted before it arrives; the stern Solim offers to take charge (CLI); Usbek agrees, and orders his wives to obey Solim (CLIII, CLIV); there is a slight lull, while Usbek reflects on his fate (CLV), then he is besieged by complaining letters from his wives (CLVI–CLVIII). Finally, we learn of Roxane's infidelity and of her death (CLIX–CLXI), and are left to imagine for ourselves the effect this news will have on Usbek.

In this series of letters, Montesquieu creates tension in three ways: he introduces events which are dramatic in themselves, such as the rebellion of the wives; he implies that fate is at work: there is the inopportune death of the chief eunuch, the unfortunate incompetence of his successor, the interception of Letter CL; and he makes us aware (through Letter CLV), that Usbek, in France, is an almost totally impotent spectator of the drama that so vitally affects him.

(iii) The characters

Skilful handling of the time-sequence and the introduction of dramatic tension are not, on their own, sufficient to make an outstanding work of fiction; in fact they are not always essential, as the example of Rousseau's letter-novel shows. An equally important ingredient for the success of a novel, at least as the term is traditionally understood, is the creation of character: the main personages must become real enough, in our imagination as readers, for us to believe in their existence; and, in the case of novels concerning a potentially tragic situation, such as we find in the *Lettres persanes*, the principal personage must be presented in such a way that he becomes a 'hero'.

That Montesquieu was aiming at psychological realism in his depiction of Usbek and Rica is evident from what he says in the 'Réflexions':

> A mesure qu'ils font un plus long séjour en Europe, les mœurs de cette partie du monde prennent dans leur tête un air moins merveilleux et moins bizarre, et ils sont plus ou moins frappés de ce bizarre et de ce merveilleux, suivant la différence de leurs caractères.

As we have seen, there is an element of self-defence in Montesquieu's insistence on the psychological aspects of the work, but that does not mean that he was insincere in this affirmation. In creating Usbek and Rica, he has succeeded in presenting us with a convincing illustration of how two people, coming from the same background, and going through similar experiences, are differentiated by their age, their health, their temperament and their personal situation.

Usbek is a wealthy Persian who, prior to the start of the story, was 'l'âme' of the intellectual élite of Ispahan, the capital (X), and who occupied an important position at court. He himself tells why he was forced to leave first the court, then the country:

> Je portai la vérité jusques au pied du trône; . . . je déconcertai la flatterie, et j'étonnai en même temps les adorateurs et l'idole [the 'idole' is the Shah].
>
> Mais, quand je vis que ma sincérité m'avait fait des ennemis; que je m'étais attiré la jalousie des ministres, sans avoir la faveur du prince; que, dans une cour corrompue, je ne me soutenais plus que par une faible vertu: je résolus de la quitter. Je feignis un grand attachement

pour les sciences, et, à force de le feindre, il me vint réellement. . . . Je me retirai dans une maison de campagne. Mais . . . je restais toujours exposé à la malice de mes ennemis. . . . Je résolus de m'exiler de ma patrie. . . . J'allai au roi; je lui marquai l'envie que j'avais de m'instruire dans les sciences de l'Occident. . . . Je trouvai grâce devant ses yeux; je partis, et je dérobai une victime à mes ennemis. (VIII)

We see from this that the cause of Usbek's self-imposed exile is a political one. He is biding his time until his enemies die or are removed by revolution; but this has not happened by the end of the novel, and when he decides to return so as to restore order in his harem, he realizes that he will be risking his life: 'Je vais rapporter ma tête à mes ennemis' (CLV). In additon to the political motive for the exile, Montesquieu is careful to give Usbek a psychological motive—a desire to learn about the West—which, though it is apparently just a pretext in order to deceive the king, is also a genuine trait of his character, that is, one aspect of his intense curiosity about the world. As he writes to Rhédi, 'Tout m'intéresse, tout m'étonne: je suis comme un enfant' (XLVIII).

When we first meet him, however, as he journeys towards Europe, it is not his curiosity which we notice so much as his preoccupation with his wives, which manifests itself in what he describes as 'une jalousie secrète, qui me dévore' (VI). His fear of his wives' infidelity makes him write cajolingly or menacingly to them (XX, XXVI, LXV) and sternly to his eunuchs (II, XXI). It remains a permanent feature of his character throughout his stay in Europe; it is the main cause of his interest in the behaviour of French women, and in particular of his condemnation of their immodesty (e.g. XXVI); it becomes intense at the close of the novel, as he orders the punishment of his unfaithful wives (CXLVIII).

Yet this same man, who is a tyrant in his private life, is, in other respects, a gentle and highly rational person, who believes that virtue is the result of individual and collective moral effort, not of constraint (XII–XIV), that honour flourishes only when personal and political liberty are respected (LXXXIX), that political power is most perfect when it uses the least violence (LXXX), and who condemns completely, in Letter CXIV, the very system of polygamous marriage which he seeks to perpetuate by maintaining a harem in Persia in spite of his absence. It could be argued that such a contradiction is implausible, and that Montesquieu lacked psychological penetration.

But Racine had already shown what we all know deep down, that passion makes people think and act in ways that are quite foreign to their rational nature. In Usbek's case the passion is jealousy, and it is for him a more permanent passion than love, since it is not directed towards one individual, but towards a group which will not change in essence, though the people who compose it may change, until he dies. Furthermore, jealousy is in a sense justified by the religion in which Usbek was brought up, where both polygamy and female chastity are important elements. Besides studying passion, Montesquieu is examining the effect of education on belief and behaviour, and indicating that rational and irrational elements can coexist within the same individual.

Usbek is a middle-aged man, with many of the habits and prejudices that this can imply, transported to a different world. His health is poor; at first, his spirit is dejected and he not surprisingly feels homesick (XXVII). So, whereas Rica's first letters from Paris are full of sprightly remarks and satirical comments on a wide variety of subjects, Usbek's are more serious in tone and in content, and often related to his own anxieties. These anxieties never entirely disappear, but his curiosity about Europe soon pushes them into the background. Nevertheless, he takes a long time to reach conclusions, and is much more tentative than Rica, whose vivacity of mind 'fait qu'il saisit tout avec promptitude. Pour moi,' continues Usbek, in a letter to Ibben, 'Pour moi, qui pense plus lentement, je ne suis en état de te rien dire' (XXV). In spite of this apparent slowness, however, he is fond of reflection, and it is he, rather than Rica, who reaches most of the conclusions about serious matters such as the nature of political power or of religion. But, for all his interest in European institutions, he never becomes completely Europeanized, and in the end we find him writing 'Je vis dans un climat barbare' (CLV), a statement which is partly occasioned by events at the harem, but which is also indicative of his deep feelings about the land of his exile.

Rica is a younger man, with no personal attachments in the country he leaves, apart from a mother who is 'inconsolable' at his departure (V), a situation which does not seem to worry him unduly. He has no harem, he does not leave Persia under pressure but (presumably) because he wishes to learn about the world in the company of a person whose intelligence he admires and whose friendship he values. His health is good: 'la force de sa constitution,' says Usbek, 'sa jeunesse et sa gaieté naturelle le mettent au-dessus de toutes les épreuves' (XXVII).

In his very first letter, he admits that he is not versed enough in European 'mœurs' and 'coutumes' to judge them properly, but this does not prevent him from going on to make witty and ironical remarks about the power of the French monarch and of the Pope (**XXIV**), and about the Catholic religion (**XXIX**). The greater part of the social satire, and of the wit, comes from his pen. He enjoys the social life of Paris, 'cette ville enchanteresse', as he calls it (**LVIII**), and he gradually, as he himself realizes, adopts Western attitudes: 'Mon esprit perd insensiblement tout ce qui lui reste d'asiatique, et se plie sans effort aux mœurs européennes' (**LXIII**). In the end, as Usbek says, 'il semble qu'il ait oublié sa patrie' (**CLV**).

Nevertheless, there are traces in him of a contradiction also found in Usbek, namely the coexistence of rationalism and superstition. Although he likes to mock religion, we find him admitting, in Letter **CXLIII**: 'Je porte toujours sur moi plus de deux mille passages du saint Alcoran; j'attache à mes bras un petit paquet où sont écrits les noms de plus de deux cents dervis.' In the same letter, however, he implies that such superstitious practices are a sign of credulity, and we conclude once more that Montesquieu is indicating that even enlightened people can be superstitious in some respects (though it could be argued that he has temporarily 'forgotten' about Rica's character, in order to indulge in satire). Among other characteristics of Rica is pity for those who are suffering—or rather Rica *says* he feels such pity (**CXXVI**): Montesquieu hints that this trait is not entirely genuine, for Rica apparently shows little sympathy for Usbek at the end of the story (**CLV**).

The two principal characters in the *Lettres persanes* are delineated quite fully and subtly. But this does not altogether answer the question of how far they take on for us that 'reality' which is essential if we are to believe in them and in their story.

It is sometimes said that people reveal themselves less by what they say about themselves than by what they say about the world around them, in that what a person says about himself is often an effort to convince himself and others of something which he would like to be true. If this is so, then Rica and Usbek, who say comparatively little about themselves but who have much to say about the society they inhabit, could be said to reveal themselves more convincingly than, for example, the hero of a novel of self-analysis, written in the first person. As we read Rica's descriptions of Parisian society, we gain a very clear picture of his geniality, his occasional superficiality, his quick wit and his cynicism. Similarly, we soon become aware, as we read Usbek's letters, that, like Rica, he is genial, but that he is more reserved, that his reflections are more mature, that he is sceptical rather than cynical, but that in certain areas he has very definite opinions, as well as deep passions and prejudices.

Thus, insofar as they are observers reacting to Parisian life, both Rica and Usbek seem to emerge as credible human beings. But are they 'heroes' in the literary sense?

In the case of Rica the answer is, definitely not. His integration into French society is completely successful, and causes no emotional conflicts in him: there is nothing here to make us feel involved, especially as we do not see him making personal contacts, of friendship or of love, with any French people.

With Usbek, it is different. Though, like Rica, he does not form any emotional ties in France, he does react emotionally to certain aspects of French life. This element of his character is portrayed skilfully, and we are able to understand, and to a certain extent sympathize with, his situation as an exile who cannot forget his country and his wives. However, if he is to become a hero, then we must be able to be deeply concerned about his predicament at the end of the novel, where he feels betrayed by those in whom he has placed his trust, and is about to return in order to punish them, thus risking his life.

Whether we feel concerned by the fate of a fictional character depends on what sort of stature he acquires in our mind, and on what causes his suffering. It seems to be a feature of Western literature that a principal character can perform foolish, even criminal and despicable acts, and still retain our interest and admiration if he is shown as a person endowed to an exceptional degree with certain basically admirable qualities such as courage, determination or sensibility; our concern is especially aroused if his actions are motivated by the passion of love.

The example of the sultan Orosmane in Voltaire's tragedy Zaïre (1732) illustrates this notion of the hero. He is shown to be an admirable ruler with a strong sense of justice; but, imagining that Zaïre, to whom he is betrothed, has been unfaithful, he stabs her in a fit of jealous rage; when he learns that she had not after all been unfaithful, he kills himself in remorse. The audience feels pity for this passionate but misguided man, even before his suicide.

Usbek is no Orosmane. He has told us that he feels no love for his wives:

Ce qui afflige le plus mon cœur, ce sont mes femmes . . .

Ce n'est pas . . . que je les aime: je me trouve à cet égard dans une insensibilité qui ne me laisse point de désirs. Dans le nombreux sérail où j'ai vécu, j'ai prévenu l'amour et l'ai détruit par lui-même. (VI)

It is of course possible that Montesquieu is hinting that Usbek is deceiving himself, and that his jealousy is a mask for his love of Roxane. If this is so, the hint is only very slight. If we judge by his letters, we do not see much evidence of love: when he writes to Roxane, he talks confidently of her love and alludes to his desires, but makes no mention of his love (XXVI); in his last letter, the predominant passions are those of self-pity, revenge and fear (CLV).

We thus assume that his suffering is caused primarily by what he feels as an affront to his rights as a harem-owner. His lack of love and his egoism finally alienate our sympathy, as does his failure to realize that his principles of rationalism and moderation are in contradiction with his emotional behaviour. Consequently, he does not achieve the stature of a hero.

We may perhaps conclude that the *Lettres persanes* contain an interesting and convincing psychological study of the changes brought about in people through the effects of time and environment, and that the harem story is told with considerable expertise, but that these two elements cannot be said to make the work into a successful novel of passion, since it lacks a proper hero. However, this fact is not detrimental to our enjoyment of the book unless (which seems unlikely) we had imagined, as we read, that Usbek was going to become a sort of tragic hero, and then had had our expectations disappointed.

(iv) The oriental background

The orient had been a fashionable subject with the French public since the beginning of the reign of Louis XIV, and Persia was one of the countries which had attracted the most attention. In 1676 and 1686 respectively, two French travellers, Tavernier and Chardin, had published remarkable descriptions of Persia. Between 1704 and 1717, there appeared a French translation of the now famous *Thousand and One Nights*, in which a large number of the tales are of Persian origin; the *Thousand and One Days*, of which most of the tales are Persian, was published in a French translation in 1710–12. Montesquieu was familiar with these works, and with many others, on the subject of the orient, and he drew on them in writing the *Lettres persanes*. Thus, for example, the westward journey of Usbek and Rica is almost the mirror image of Tavernier's journey east; Montesquieu's information about harems comes largely from Chardin, who emphasizes, for instance, the extreme modesty of Persian brides (see Letter XXVI, § 1), the severity of the restrictions imposed on the wives and concubines (see Letter VII, § 2), and the prevalence of lesbianism (see Letter IV), and whose description of the life of the eunuchs is the source of Letter IX.

However, the picture we get of Usbek's harem is not a compilation. Montesquieu has so thoroughly assimilated his sources that he has created an atmosphere which, while it may not be strictly authentic, is nevertheless very convincing. This is apparent as early as Letter II, which Usbek writes to the chief eunuch, and which is characterized by an evocative use of imagery, and by antithesis:

> Tu es le gardien fidèle des plus belles femmes de Perse; . . . Tu fais la garde dans le silence de la nuit, comme dans le tumulte du jour. . . . Tu es le fléau du vice et la colonne de la fidélité.

In this same letter, as in others (III, IX), we learn something of the practical side of life in a harem: Usbek tells the chief eunuch to grant the wives

> tous les plaisirs qui peuvent être innocents; trompe leurs inquiétudes; amuse-les par la musique, les danses, les boissons délicieuses; persuade-leur de s'assembler souvent. Si elles veulent aller à la campagne, tu peux les y mener; mais fais main basse sur tous les hommes qui se présenteront devant elles. Exhorte-les à la propreté, qui est l'image de la netteté de l'âme. (II)

We see something of Persian customs of marriage (LXX–LXXI) and its consummation, often a protracted process (XXVI); and of the way children are brought up (LXII). There is a very full account of the thoughts and feelings of the eunuchs, who exercise great power, and who live in the constant awareness of the deprivation they have suffered in order to achieve it. Letter IX, from the chief eunuch, is a fascinating psychological study. Having recounted the circumstances of the sacrifice of his masculinity, he dwells on the mental effects of the operation: 'Hélas! on éteignit en moi l'effect des passions, sans en éteindre la cause et, bien loin d'en être soulagé, je me trouvai environné d'objets qui les irritaient sans cesse.' He describes the indignities he has suffered from the women he commands, and continues:

Enfin, les feux de la jeunesse ont passé; je suis vieux, et je me trouve à cet égard dans un état tranquille; je regarde les femmes avec indifférence, et je leur rends bien tous leurs mépris. . . . Je me souviens toujours que j'étais né pour les commander, et il me semble que je redeviens homme dans les occasions où je leur commande encore. Je les hais depuis que je les envisage de sens froid. . . .

Montesquieu is clearly interested in the mental effects of the physical change undergone by the eunuchs, and his picture of their lives is both plausible and intriguing.

Equally strong but more conventional emotions are found in the depiction of the passions of the wives and concubines. We see the jealous competition for the attentions of the master (III, XCVI), the compensations sought by those who are disdained, namely lesbianism (IV), or, if the conditions become sufficiently lax, the taking of a lover (CLI). The language in which these emotions are conveyed is dignified and rhetorical: 'Mais où suis-je!' exclaims Zachi to Usbek, having recounted her former days of glory as favourite wife:

Où m'emmène ce vain récit? C'est un malheur de n'être point aimée; mais c'est un affront de ne l'être plus. . . . Je pousse des soupirs qui ne sont point entendus; mes larmes coulent, et tu n'en jouis pas; il semble que l'amour respire dans le sérail, et ton insensibilité t'en éloigne sans cesse! Ah! mon cher Usbek, si tu savais être heureux. (III)

The passionate atmosphere of the harem is conveyed quite successfully. But are the inmates of the harem credible human beings? It is difficult to answer this question, as very few of Usbek's wives have more than a single letter; there is in fact more continuity as regards the chief eunuch, who writes several, and reveals much about himself. The only two women who emerge as characters are Fatmé and Roxane. Fatmé writes only one letter, but it is marked by a veiled irony which lifts its writer out of the artificial category of *la femme délaissée* to which Zachi belongs. Fatmé begins her letter to Usbek by lamenting his departure; she appears deeply distressed by it, and proclaims her fidelity; but in the third paragraph, her language changes from the sentimental to the sensual, in a way which hints that she is finding satisfactions (of an unspecified nature) without her husband, and the letter ends with an outspoken and cynical comment on masculine vanity:

Vous êtes bien cruels, vous autres hommes! Vous êtes charmés que nous ayons des passions que nous ne puissions satisfaire; vous nous traitez comme si nous étions insensibles, et vous seriez bien fâchés que nous le fussions; vous croyez que nos désirs, si longtemps mortifiés, seront irrités à votre vue. Il y a de la peine à se faire aimer; il est plus court d'obtenir du désespoir de nos sens ce que vous n'osez attendre de votre mérite. (VII)

The tone points us towards the conclusion of the story, but Fatmé writes no more letters and we lose sight of her. The combination of eroticism and feminism which is found in Fatmé's letter is characteristic of some of the other letters too, particularly of Letter CXLI (in which Rica tells the story of the revenge taken by Anaïs on her jealous and brutal husband Ibrahim), and feminism without eroticism is a marked feature of the last letter of Roxane, Usbek's favourite wife.

Roxane is the only one of the wives who has a recognizable character and plays a significant part in the ending of the story. Just before she dies, she writes to Usbek, proclaiming her physical and moral revolt against his domination, and vividly expressing her anger and resentment:

Oui, je t'ai trompé; j'ai séduit tes eunuques, je me suis jouée de ta jalousie, et j'ai su, de ton affreux sérail, faire un lieu de délices et de plaisirs. . . .

Comment as-tu pensé que je fusse assez crédule pour m'imaginer que je ne fusse dans le monde que pour adorer tes caprices? que, pendant que tu te permets tout, tu eusses le droit d'affliger tous mes désirs? Non! J'ai pu vivre dans la servitude, mais j'ai toujours été libre: j'ai réformé tes lois sur celles de la Nature. . . . (CLXI)

These words have the effect of making us sympathize more with the spirited woman who wrote them than with her domineering husband, thus underlining the fact that Usbek is not to be seen as a hero; but we do not see enough of Roxane for her to become any kind of tragic heroine. This reinforces the conclusion that it was not Montesquieu's purpose, in writing about the harem, to produce a deeply-moving story. His first and least important aim must have been to interest his readers by an exciting story set in an exotic world and enlivened by eroticism; the second, to provide a framework for certain psychological observations; the third, to give a practical demonstration of one of the truths he wished to convey in the work, namely that repression inevitably provokes violence and revolution.

(v) The language

If the harem story is convincing (without being moving), this is largely because of the language in which it is told. Montesquieu, by employing a relatively small number of words with oriental associations, together with a majority taken from the *style noble* of seventeenth-century France, creates in our minds a world which is foreign to us in certain respects, but very familiar to us in others, with its emphasis on the passions of jealousy and love.

In the letters where the oriental style is used to convey ideas about religion, a somewhat similar procedure is used, in that the orientalisms are a sort of fancy dress in which are clothed notions belonging to the Western world. For example, in the letter which Usbek writes to Mollak Méhémet-Hali, seeking advice on religious matters:

> Ta science est un abîme plus profond que l'Océan; ton esprit est plus perçant que Zufagar, cette épée d'Hali qui avait deux pointes; tu sais ce qui se passe dans les neuf chœurs des Puissances célestes; tu lis l'Alcoran sur la poitrine de notre divin prophète. (XVI)

The reader is perhaps not very concerned with why Mahomet's son-in-law Hali or Ali had a double-pointed sword, or why there are nine heavenly choirs; he probably accepts this as the sort of language a Persian might write. But the language has another purpose. On their own, the hyperbolic compliments perhaps seem appropriate; but when we read Méhémet-Hali's reply, which strikes us as a piece of garbled nonsense, we realize that there is a satirical purpose behind Usbek's words, or, more precisely, that Montesquieu is using them in a deliberately ironical way, to indicate that Usbek still half respects things which are not worthy of respect, that there is a contradiction between his thoughts, which are already in this letter highly rationalistic, and his beliefs, which have not altered.

That it was not Montesquieu's aim simply to create, in Usbek, a convincing Persian character, but to make him, at the same time, the exponent of certain universally desirable attitudes, is indicated by the fact that the oriental style is by no means always in evidence, even when we might expect it (Montesquieu pretends, in the 'Introduction', that he has 'soulagé le lecteur du langage asiatique', and used it as little as possible). Thus most of the letters written by Usbek on philosophical subjects contain few or no orientalisms, and even when he is writing to his friends back in Persia, he uses the sort of language we would expect a French gentleman, an *honnête homme*, to use, with its subtle compliments and its self-effacement: 'Mon cher Mirza, il y a une chose qui me flatte encore plus que la bonne opinion que tu as conçue de moi: c'est ton amitié qui me la procure' (XI).

When he is talking about political or historical subjects, Usbek has a taste for comparisons belonging to the classical French style, which are often drawn from some grandiose aspect of the natural world, or of the world of man. He compares the *Parlements* to 'ces ruines que l'on foule aux pieds, mais qui rappellent toujours l'idée de quelque temple fameux . . . ' (XCII), and conquering hordes to 'des torrents impétueux' whose 'puissance aurait passé comme le bruit du tonnerre et des tempêtes' if they had not practised the arts (CVI). This sort of language was almost universal in historical writings in Montesquieu's time but fortunately, perhaps, it is not used continuously by Usbek, who is capable of talking on serious subjects in a less elevated manner, as in the story of the Troglodytes, which is allegorical, and pastoral in tone, or in the letters on the population of the world, where the style alternates between simple exposition of ideas and a very pronounced irony.

The imagery used by Montesquieu's characters is quite original. Just occasionally, a pleasing image is used to convey a pleasing idea: the extravagantly-dressed and painted French women who flock to see Rica while he is still wearing his Persian robes 'faisaient un arc-en-ciel, nuancé de mille couleurs' (XXX). More often, though, the image works by its power to evoke something disagreeable: when Montesquieu wishes to discredit the 'laquais' or *nouveaux riches* who, because of their wealth, are able to marry their daughters into impoverished noble families, in order to obtain social standing, he makes Usbek say:

> ils relèvent toutes les grandes maisons par le moyen de leurs filles, qui sont comme une espèce de fumier qui engraisse les terres montagneuses et arides. (XCVIII)

In this case, the word 'fumier' surprises us by its vulgar associations; at the same time, it underlines the mercenary attitude of the 'laquais' towards their daughters. Elsewhere, a more abstract comparison is used to discredit certain people or activities: 'J'ai vu souvent neuf ou dix femmes, ou plutôt neuf ou dix siècles rangés autour d'une table,' says Rica of the ageing women gamblers (LVI); the word 'siècles' conveys an impression of slow but dignified decay, which is grotesquely inappropriate to the women's passionate involvement in a trivial pastime. On other occasions, more concrete images are used to underline a piece of satire: the intense concern shown by Western women about their appearance is emphasized by Rica when he compares a woman putting on her make-up to a general arranging his troops for battle (CX); and pretentiousness is unmasked when a Frenchman says of the Spanish and Portuguese that their 'gravité' 'se manifeste principalement de deux manières: par les lunettes et par la moustache' (LXXVIII); the suggestion is that spectacles and mustachios are substitutes for the qualities they are supposed to represent.

Montesquieu's imagery cannot be separated from his use of irony. Irony means the discrepancy between the apparent and the real meaning of certain words; writers of eighteenth-century fiction used it in more than one way. There is 'dramatic' irony (the term is borrowed from the theatre, but càn be applied to the novel as well), which can take two forms. The first is where the author makes a character pronounce words which, besides their obvious meaning, have hidden implications of which the character is unaware, but which the reader, if he is perceptive, or if he knows the story already, can see: there is an example of this in the last paragraph of Letter XLVIII, where Usbek talks confidently but, as we realize, mistakenly of the purity of his wives. The second form of dramatic irony is where the character who is speaking is aware of the implications of his words, but where the person to whom he is addressing himself is not, for example when Usbek's wives write assuring him of their affection, when in fact they hate him. In both cases, the function of the irony is dramatic in that it increases the tension created in the reader by the situation in which the principal character is involved.

Besides dramatic irony, there is another kind of irony which, although it has similar characteristics, serves a different purpose, that of criticizing an idea, a custom, or an institution. It may be described as 'intellectual' irony, and can be indirect or direct. When a character says something which he wishes the person to whom he is speaking to take seriously, but which the author intends the reader to understand in a different sense, we have indirect intellectual irony; here, the character seems to be unaware of the critical implications of his words. This is probably the case with Usbek's compliments to priests; in another example of the same kind of irony, the reader has a certain amount of work to do before he discerns the author's intention. Usbek says:

Il y a dans notre Alcoran un grand nombre de petites choses qui me paraissent toujours telles, quoiqu'elles soient relevées par la force et la vie de l'expression. . . . Dans notre Alcoran, on trouve souvent le langage de Dieu et les idées des hommes. (XCVII)

Here there is direct criticism of the Koran and implied criticism of the Bible; the direct criticism is made by Usbek, but the implied criticism seems to come from Montesquieu rather than Usbek, since it is unlikely that the Persian is sufficiently familiar with the style of the Bible to make such a judgement. When the reader recognizes this indirect irony, he probably feels a sense of pleasure at having penetrated the author's ingenuity.

In the direct form of intellectual irony, a character says something which he wishes the person to whom he is talking not to take literally; here, both he himself and the person to whom he is speaking are aware of the critical implication. When Usbek ends Letter CXVI by saying of the Christian view of marriage: 'c'est une image, une figure et quelque chose de mystérieux que je ne comprends point', he is not really, as he pretends, refraining from judging the idea that marriage represents the mystical union between Christ and his Church, but inviting Rhédi, to whom he is writing, to infer that such an incomprehensible doctrine, which has, as he has shown earlier in the letter, disastrous social consequences, is to be scorned by any rational person. This device amounts to false naïvety, and is used very frequently in the Lettres persanes.

A good example of this ironical false naïvety occurs when Rica talks of the Trinity and of transubstantiation. He pretends that he cannot see that these doctrines are meant to concern spiritual realities, and insists on applying them to ordinary reality. Thus, when he says that the Pope makes the French king think 'que trois ne sont qu'un, que le pain qu'on mange n'est pas du pain, ou que le vin qu'on boit n'est pas du vin, et mille autres choses de cette espèce', the apparent meaning is that the Pope is a 'magicien' who can play amusing conjuring tricks; but, by saying at the same time that the pontiff is 'maître' of Louis XIV's mind, Rica is in fact implying that he is a power-hungry knave, whose dominion rests on his ability to persuade people not to believe their own eyes or trust their own reason (XXIV). Rica is also implying, as was Usbek when he described the Christian view of marriage as a 'figure', that for rational people, there is no such thing as a spiritual reality distinct from ordinary reality.

A particularly piquant case of this ironical false naïvety is Usbek's habit of referring to members of European religious orders as 'dervis' (e.g. Letter LVII), which term does mean more or less 'monk' but also has associations of dancing and sword-swallowing, as well as of hypocrisy, and so tends to reflect discredit on the people to whom it is applied. Similarly, Usbek calls monks and priests 'eunuques' (CXVII), because he believes that they have forsaken what he sees as one of the first duties of every member of society, namely procreation. We have the impression that he is well aware that monks and priests are not really 'eunuques', and that he is using the term in a deliberately ironical way.

Montesquieu does not rely solely on irony, in order to entertain. Often he makes his characters use a witty style, where the intention is simply to surprise us. This is particularly true of the letters concerned with social satire. When Rica says 'Les Français ne parlent presque jamais de leurs femmes' (LV), we probably think he is going to explain the fact by showing that French husbands do not care about their wives. But no, the explanation shows them as victims rather than as victimizers: 'c'est qu'ils ont peur d'en parler devant des gens qui les connaissent mieux qu'eux.' At other times, we are surprised by being offered an unusual view of an event or custom: 'La fureur de la plupart des Français, c'est d'avoir de l'esprit, et la fureur de ceux qui veulent avoir de l'esprit, c'est de faire des livres' (LXVI). But instead of being given examples of boring witticisms and boring books, we are shown that the idea of perpetuating one's silly ideas is somehow contrary to the natural order of things:

la Nature semblait avoir sagement pourvu à ce que les sottises des hommes fussent passagères, et les livres les immortalisent.

The word 'Nature' refers, in this context and in some others (e.g. LXXIII, § 5), to simplicity and unaffected behaviour, although it has deeper meanings as well.[6] The idea of simplicity is itself one of the main criteria of the social satire found in the Lettres persanes.

[6] This subject is very clearly explained by R. Grimsley in 'The idea of nature in Montesquieu's Lettres persanes' (see 'Suggestions for Further Reading').

3. The Lettres persanes *as Social Satire*

The standpoint of Montesquieu the satirist is fairly traditional. It has usually been the aim of satirists to discredit not only vice but also excessive sophistication and unusual social behaviour, both by direct criticism and by ridicule. This kind of satire is referred to as *social satire*, and it is helpful to distinguish it from *political satire* (although in practice it is not always possible to separate the two), which implies criticism not so much of the manners or vices of individuals as of political and legal institutions, and which evokes much wider issues. The political ideas of the *Lettres persanes*, which are sometimes presented satirically, will be examined later. As a preliminary to the understanding of both the political satire and the social satire, it is necessary to know something of the world which Montesquieu is looking at through the keen eyes of his Persians.

Rica and Usbek arrive in Paris towards the beginning of May 1712. At this date, Louis XIV, 'le plus puissant prince de l'Europe', as Rica calls him (XXIV), had been on the throne for sixty-eight years, and for the last fifty years he had ruled personally. During his reign he exercised an authority which his enemies abroad, and certain of his own subjects, saw as absolute. Modern historians have shown that this is an exaggeration, but it was certainly his aim to centralize the government of France, and to remove from the bodies which had up till then shared some power with the monarch (namely the *Parlements*, or law-courts, and the aristocracy) their political privileges, many of which dated back to feudal times.

Another of Louis's aims was to increase France's prestige abroad, both by military action and by encouraging the arts. Until about 1685, he was successful in this respect, but after that date he began to be hampered by financial difficulties, and his expansionist foreign policy met with increasing opposition from abroad. In the last years of his reign, circumstances worsened still further: there was a run of defeats in war and a series of bad harvests; the national debt increased enormously; and there were several deaths in the royal family. These adversities, coupled with Louis XIV's growing concern with the afterlife (fostered by the woman to whom he was secretly married, madame de Maintenon, and by some of his ministers), introduced an atmosphere of gloom into a court which in earlier years had been the scene of every kind of profusion and magnificence, and the European centre of artistic creation.

When Louis XIV died, in 1715, there was no adult prince to succeed him, and the throne was occupied by his great-grandson, aged five (see Letter XCII). The government was placed in the hands of a regent, Philippe d'Orléans, nephew to Louis XIV. He delegated some of his power to a number of councils, and to the *Parlement* of Paris, in order to strengthen his position by inviting the co-operation of those who might otherwise have been opposed to him. The Regency, which lasted till 1723, was marked by a reaction against the restraints on behaviour which had prevailed in the later years of Louis XIV, a reaction in which the Regent himself set the example. It was also marked by further financial problems: the government of Louis XIV had left a huge deficit, which the Regent tried to wipe out, first by attempting to bully the financiers, who were popularly imagined to have caused the country's poverty (it is true that they were partly responsible for it, since it was they who ran France's inefficient and inequitable system for gathering indirect taxes, but there were other causes, such as military overspending); and then by listening to John Law, a Scotsman with a scheme for abolishing the deficit by increasing commercial activity, which would supposedly result in greater prosperity and in an increase in government revenue. Law's *système*, as it was called, though fairly sound in itself, was applied without sufficient caution, and led to a period of massive inflation and speculation, which ruined many aristocrats, and enriched many people without title. This great social change, deplored in the *Lettres persanes* (CXLVI), may have been beneficial in that it ran counter to the general trend towards domination of the country by a few select and long-established families.

The period over which the action of the *Lettres persanes* takes place was characterized by social mobility, and, after 1715, by a certain degree of personal and intellectual freedom (censorship of books was less rigidly enforced during the 1720s than before or after). It represents that taste of freedom after repression which often provokes revolution—in this case a revolution which, though almost immediate in its intellectual aspects, was delayed in political fact for some seventy years.

The *Lettres persanes* reflect the passing of the old order and the start of the new. We learn something of the nature of the power exercised by the old king, and of the changes wrought by his death; we meet a whole gallery of people who, though unusual in themselves, typify the variegated character of the society in which Montesquieu lived. When some individual characteristic or social usage merely contravenes the idea of simplicity or commonsense, the satirist (usually it is Rica) adopts a bantering or lightly mocking tone. When characteristics or usages are shown to have unpleasant social consequences, the tone becomes serious, even indignant; this is particularly the case with some of Usbek's letters.

On the whole, when we are shown, through the letters of Rica and Usbek, the principal features of the French as a people, it is the mocking rather than the indignant tone which predominates. The characteristic which immediately strikes Rica is the curiosity that the French show towards anything with which they are unfamiliar, in this case the strangely-dressed Persians. Rica thinks that the curiosity is based on surprise rather than on genuine interest, because, when he decides to 'quitter l'habit persan et à en endosser un à l'européenne', he finds he is completely ignored. The only reaction he can obtain, if he tells people he is Persian, is an expression of bewilderment: 'Ah! ah! Monsieur est Persan? c'est une chose bien extraordinaire! Comment peut-on être Persan?' (XXX). This insularity is underlined by Usbek in Letter XLVIII:

> Notre air étranger n'offense plus personne; nous jouissons même de la surprise où l'on est de nous trouver quelque politesse: car les Français n'imaginent pas que notre climat produise des hommes.

So much for the satire; Usbek then adds: 'Cependant, il faut l'avouer, ils valent la peine qu'on les détrompe.' And although we see comparatively little of such attempts to *détromper* the French (for Usbek is a modest man), his words are indicative of his friendly attitude, which cools only when the situation in the harem becomes disastrous. Usbek is thus shown as being more truly interested in the French than they are in him. Rica's attitude is more critical: he implies, for instance, that the sympathy often displayed by the French towards each other is somewhat hypocritical, witness the indefatigable Frenchman he instances who, in his lifetime, went to 530 funerals and who sent 2,680 letters of congratulation to parents of newly-born children (LXXXVII).

The satire of certain cultural institutions is an important element in the work: we learn, through an ingenious extended metaphor, of the lethargy and dullness of the French Academy (LXXIII); the Sorbonne is mocked for its concern with futile religious disputes (CIX); we are treated to a description of the theatre, which mystifies us until we realize that Rica is talking not of the actors on the stage, who are clearly not very important, but of the *jeux de scène* of the members of the audience, who go not to watch a play, but to see their friends or lovers, and to be seen (XXVIII); we are shown into a *café*, a relatively new feature of Parisian life, where *les beaux esprits* go to discuss trivial literary matters (XXXVI), and we meet a group of 'nouvellistes' (journalists—the newspaper was a comparatively recent innovation) who gather in the Tuileries to exchange news and conjecture (CXXX); there is a satirical account of the literary journals of the day, which, in their book reviews, tended to avoid making any criticisms, and were consequently rather dull (CVIII); and in Letters CXXXIV–CXXXVII there is a long description of the contents of a library with somewhat naïvely satirical comments—here Rica's verve temporarily dries up.

Many of the wittiest letters satirize the behaviour of representative individuals. In the eighteenth century, social success often depended on wit. There is an illustration of this in Letter LIV, in which Rica recounts how he overheard two would-be brilliant conversationalists discussing how they might overcome their failure to shine in company by discreet mutual help in introducing jokes. A predominant feature of intellectual life at the time was the stress laid on the study of the sciences. Letter CXXVIII gives us a portrait of the 'géomètre' (the mathematician) who has become so obsessed with his subject that he sees everything in the world about him in terms of geometrical figures, and who, when he absentmindedly bumps into a passer-by, feels no pain, but merely calculates the physical forces which have been brought into play. The portrait is exaggerated, of course, but behind the exaggeration Montesquieu is pointing to a truth about human psychology, namely, the idiosyncratic nature of the individual's view of the world.

There is mockery of various features of Parisian life, particularly of gambling (LVI), and of fashions, which change so fast and which seem, viewed through Rica's vivid imagination, to transform human anatomy, and even the shape of buildings:

> Quelquefois, les coiffures montent insensiblement, et une révolution les fait descendre tout à coup. Il a été un temps que leur hauteur immense mettait le visage d'une femme au milieu d'elle-même. Dans un autre, c'étaient les pieds qui occupaient cette place: les talons faisaient un piédestal qui les tenait en l'air. Qui pourrait le croire? Les architectes ont été souvent obligés de hausser, de baisser et d'élargir

leurs portes, selon que les parures des femmes exigeaient d'eux ce changement. (XCIX)

Here, as elsewhere, the *Lettres persanes* give evidence of a trend which had begun in the seventeenth century, but developed considerably in the eighteenth, namely the influence of women on many aspects of public life. Rica stresses the role they play in politics:

> Il n'y a personne qui ait quelque emploi à la Cour, dans Paris ou dans les provinces, qui n'ait une femme par les mains de laquelle passent toutes les grâces et quelquefois les injustices qu'il peut faire. Ces femmes ont toutes des relations les unes avec les autres et forment une espèce de république . . . . : c'est comme un nouvel État dans l'État. . . .
>
> Crois-tu, Ibben, qu'une femme s'avise d'être la maîtresse d'un ministre pour coucher avec lui? Quelle idée! C'est pour lui présenter cinq ou six placets tous les matins. (CVII)

Rica betrays, in these words, a certain disapproval, but it probably arises from his dislike of unfairness, and not from any anti-feminist prejudice, since elsewhere he is remarkably open-minded about women: in Letter XXXVIII, he openly questions the subordinate position accorded to them in the orient, and his comments on feminine coquetry (CX) and adultery (LV) (which according to contemporary moralists were prevalent, not to say fashionable) have few moral overtones.

When it is Usbek who is writing about French women, there is little of the lighthearted mockery which characterizes Rica's letters on the subject. Instead, there is moral condemnation, often coupled with what appears to be subconscious fear. This reaction is particularly obvious in the letter he writes to Roxane, alluding to the 'impudence brutale' of society women, but earnestly denying that they are ever unfaithful to their husbands (XXVI). The same reaction is evident when he meets men who present a threat to female virtue, such as the 'homme à bonnes fortunes' (the libertine), for whom he deems castration to be a suitable punishment, and the lax priest, who encourages his women penitents to sacrifice their chastity, because he enjoys sinning by proxy, thus betraying his function as a moral counsellor (XLVIII).

Usbek has social as well as moral prejudices, as we see in his condemnation of the *fermier*. The *fermiers*, or tax-collectors, were men with sufficient wealth to pay the nearly bankrupt government large sums of money in exchange for the right to raise certain indirect taxes; they were often of comparatively low birth, and were frequently seen as boorish social climbers. The aristocratic Usbek shares this view: he describes the *fermier* he sees as being uneducated and as having 'la physionomie si basse qu'il ne fait guère honneur aux gens de qualité' (XLVIII).

Apart from the social reasons which determine Usbek's view of the *fermier*, there is another cause at work, his dislike of vanity: the *fermier* boasts about the banquets he has given, speaks in a loud voice, and is very pleased with himself. Rica has a similar aversion to vanity (L, CXLIV), and some of his most entertaining sketches satirize this trait: there are the four women who, in response to his adroit questions, reveal their fond belief in their youthfulness (LII); and there is the 'décisionnaire' (the know-all), 'un homme bien content de lui', who, 'dans un quart d'heure . . . décida trois questions de morale, quatre problèmes historiques et cinq points de physique' (LXXII).

Besides this vanity produced by an individual's high opinion of himself, there is the vanity which results from social status: each of the three social orders (*états*) in France 'a un mépris souverain pour les deux autres' (XLIV), an attitude exemplified by 'un grand seigneur qui est un des hommes du royaume qui représente le mieux' (*représenter*, here, means to try to impress others). Usbek describes him with a wealth of significant behavioural details which betray his vanity:

> Je vis un petit homme si fier, il prit une prise de tabac avec tant de hauteur, il se moucha si impitoyablement, il cracha avec tant de flegme, il caressa ses chiens d'une manière si offensante pour les hommes, que je ne pouvais me lasser de l'admirer. (LXXIV)

Finally, there is the vanity displayed, usually unconsciously, by men in general, in that they believe themselves to be the centre of the universe, when in fact they are merely a very insignificant part of it; this attitude is particularly pronounced when they are reflecting on the subject of their own death, which they consider to be a major catastrophe. Usbek prefers to see human life in a wider perspective:

> nous ne sentons point notre petitesse, et, malgré qu'on en ait, nous voulons être comptés dans l'Univers, y figurer et y être un objet important. Nous nous imaginons que l'anéantissement d'un être aussi parfait que nous dégraderait toute la nature, et nous ne convenons pas qu'un homme de plus ou de moins dans le monde—que dis-je?—tous les hommes ensemble . . . ne sont qu'un atome subtil et délié. . . . (LXXVI)

Here, once more, Montesquieu is underlining, through Usbek, the one-sided nature of man's view of himself and of the universe.

The social satire in the *Lettres persanes* surprises us by its breadth and variety. It covers a great many of the important aspects of eighteenth-century French society in Paris, though it is true that there is little about the life and manners of the lower classes, such a subject being rarely alluded to in the literature of the period, and little about servants. There is a frequent element of exaggeration in the satirical descriptions of manners, but the exaggeration is of an imaginative kind which helps us vividly to picture the society evoked for us, with its feverish social activities, its desires and dreams (usually connected with money), its hypocrisies, its successful people, its cranks and its outcasts. Political freedom, at that time, may have been almost non-existent, but personal freedom was often in evidence.

In spite of the variety of viewpoint and mood evident in the social satire, we become aware, as we read, of certain constant attitudes on the part of the characters, attitudes which seem to indicate a philosophical standpoint on the part of the author; and when we close the book, we become aware that Montesquieu has put forward, both through the satire and more directly in the philosophical letters, a consistent view of how men should live their lives as individuals and as members of society, and of how society might be better organized to achieve a greater degree of political freedom and political stability.

4. Philosophical Elements in the Lettres persanes

Montesquieu's 'philosophy' (the word is to be understood in the sense defined on p. 9) in the *Lettres persanes* falls into two categories. First there is his view of man's relation, as an individual, to the physical and social world around him; this view constitutes what may be called the general principles of his philosophy. Secondly, there is his view of the two sets of institutions which shape men's lives, religion and politics.

(i) *Montesquieu's philosophical principles*

The principles of Montesquieu's philosophy can be summarized under three headings: relativism, belief in reason, and belief in justice and morality. The second and third of these principles are in apparent contradiction with the first, but it will be shown that this is not in fact the case.

Relativism can be defined as the belief that human judgements are subjective, that is, based on the way we perceive the world through our senses, and on the way we interpret those perceptions. It is the opposite of what philosophers call 'realism', which is the belief that there exist certain immutable and absolute standards (of beauty, or justice, for example) of which man can be aware innately or intuitively, or which he may accept on authority.

Although they do not actually use the word 'relativism', Rica and Usbek are both relativists. Towards the end of an amusing letter in which he has given examples of how people tend to see things from their own point of view, Rica concludes:

> nous ne jugeons jamais des choses que par un retour secret que nous faisons sur nous-mêmes. (LIX)

The same idea is put more philosophically in Letter XVII, where

Usbek argues against the belief, found in various religions, that certain objects are inherently impure; he claims that purity and impurity are not qualities in objects, but merely judgements made by ourselves, through our senses. What he says about impurity can be applied, by analogy, to all the judgements we make: all are relative. His awareness of man's dependence on his senses is confirmed when he hears an atheist saying: 'Je crois l'immortalité de l'âme par semestre; mes opinions dépendent absolument de la constitution de mon corps' (LXXV).

What Usbek says about individual judgements may also be true of judgements made by whole nations, and in fact one of Montesquieu's main aims, in the *Lettres persanes*, is to show how different societies produce different standards of judgement and of behaviour, and how each tends to think that these standards are absolute. Montesquieu underlines the relativity of such standards: what the Persian accepts as normal, for example the use of eunuchs as guardians in the harem, strikes the European as both wrong and foolish (XXXIV); the Catholic may believe that salvation is possible only within the Church, but the Moslem is shown to have a similar prejudice about *his* religion (XXXV); a Frenchman may imagine that the political system of his country is immensely superior to that of the orient (CIII), but it is suggested that the two systems are not altogether dissimilar (XXXVII).

The aim behind these implicit and explicit comparisons is to make us abandon our own complacency. The question which Rica is asked, 'Comment peut-on être Persan?' (XXX), is amusing in its own right as a satire of the French, but Montesquieu would like us to take the matter further and apply it not so much to others, as to ourselves, and to ask: 'What is the justification of our own moral, political and religious beliefs?' It is true that, in the end, Montesquieu's own prejudices sometimes emerge, for example when he implies that certain European beliefs and practices are superior, but this does not mean that the question was not worth asking. In arriving at his assessment of European societies, he has been able to challenge many dubious assumptions.

We see that Montesquieu has a positive purpose in mind when he stresses the subjectivity of our judgements. His relativism does not result in scepticism, for he is not saying that all judgements are equally false or that we have no means of arriving at the truth. He believes that we can reach it through our reason, which he seems to consider to be a faculty distinct from, and capable of rising above, judgement.

Montesquieu's belief in reason as a valid instrument in the discovery of truth should be seen in the perspective of previous and contemporary attitudes.

Confidence in reason, which was one of the principal features of the Renaissance and of the early seventeenth century, was attacked in Pascal's *Pensées* (1670), a work of religious apology which tried to show (among other things) that man's reason, being almost totally corrupt since the Fall, cannot arrive at the truth, which is knowable only through Revelation. However, Pascal's anti-rationalism was an anachronism: the seventeenth century saw many important developments in the physical sciences and in mathematics (some of them paradoxically brought about by Pascal himself, who in his earlier years had been an outstanding scientist). Forward-looking philosophers, particularly Descartes, believed that reason, properly directed, could reach the truth about the natural world, and eventually control it too; he also believed that human psychology could be subjected to rational analysis, but, being a cautious man, he deliberately excluded from his investigations the moral, political and religious standards of his country.

Such timidity Montesquieu, like most eighteenth-century thinkers, was to disdain, but he, and they, did this not by denying Descartes's method, but by applying it more consistently than he himself had done. We see, in the *Lettres persanes*, that Montesquieu believes human reason to be potentially capable of explaining all natural phenomena, and all human phenomena as well, whether legal, social, historical or moral.

His confidence in reason as an instrument of scientific investigation emerges clearly from Letter XCVII, written by Usbek. It is an enthusiastic account of the achievements of Descartes and his successors, who, by following 'les traces de la raison humaine', have 'débrouillé le Chaos', and reduced the apparent complexity of the natural world to a few simple laws of physics.

In the same letter, Usbek contrasts the constancy and simplicity of the laws of the natural world with the changeable laws of 'les sociétés des hommes'. However, this is not, as it might appear, a denial of the possibility of investigating human laws, since he relates their apparent irrationality to causes which could be studied and analysed, namely 'l'esprit de ceux qui les proposent, et des peuples qui les observent'. He takes the matter no further in this letter, but in Letters CXIV–CXXII, his concern is precisely to make a rational study of the interrelation between the way people think and act, and the institutions which govern them; in other letters, he shows how laws might be better adapted to their task of ensuring public order (CXXXIX), or made more just (XCV). Rica, who sometimes surprises us by being more profound than he appears, pursues a similar enterprise in Letter C, where he looks at the origin and development of law, and in the important Letter CXLIII, where he argues that all historical events can be explained rationally.

Montesquieu, in his study of human law, is intensely interested in the question of its justice, which term is to be understood as the rightness of certain actions or institutions, viewed from the point of view of the community as a whole; he is equally concerned with morality, which is the rightness of certain actions, viewed from the point of view of the individual in his relations with his fellow men and with society. Justice and morality, for Montesquieu, are simply two aspects of the same idea, and he sees both in a rationalistic manner.

This rationalistic conception of justice and morality is to be found above all in Letter LXXXIII, written by Usbek. Its central position in the structure of the work underlines its central position in Montesquieu's philosophical outlook.

> La Justice est un rapport de convenance, qui se trouve réellement entre deux choses; ce rapport est toujours le même, quelque être qui le considère, soit que ce soit Dieu, soit que ce soit un ange, ou enfin que ce soit un homme.

In this rather complicated definition, Usbek seems to be saying that rational beings ('Dieu, . . . un homme') can determine the rightness or wrongness of any action by examining the particular nature of the 'choses' (namely, men and society) involved. Justice, or morality, is 'un rapport de convenance' (literally, a relationship implying what is right or appropriate in given circumstances) because it is based on the relationships between one citizen and another, and between the citizen and the society he lives in.

This idea of justice reveals at the same time Usbek's rationalism and his relativism: his rationalism, because justice is discovered almost mathematically or statistically, through the application of the reason to the particular 'choses' under consideration: all thinking beings will, if they disregard their prejudices, arrive at the same conclusions from the same data ('ce rapport est toujours le même, quelque être qui le considère'); his relativism, because justice can never be absolute, that is, the same for all times and all places, since the nature of the 'choses' from which it is derived varies in certain respects (though it could be the same in two countries, if conditions in them were identical). As a relativist, Usbek warns against thinking that what is merely the prejudice of a community constitutes justice, by affirming 'la Justice ... ne dépend point des conventions humaines'.[1]

Usbek does not, in Letter LXXXIII, give examples of these *rapports de convenance*, and consequently his idea seems somewhat abstract and vague. However, in Letter XLVI he puts forward three laws of justice and morality which, he says, should govern the behaviour of the citizen: 'l'observation des lois, l'amour pour les hommes, la piété envers les parents' (he calls these 'les premiers actes de religion', but the context makes it clear that he sees them as acts of morality). Are these, perhaps, examples of *rapports de convenance*? The second rule is rather general, and is best left out of the discussion. The first, 'l'observation des lois', can be interpreted thus: the citizen's relationship with society seems to be one of dependence—he has to obey the law, pay taxes, fight for his country; one might say that his existence is of advantage to society. However, in that his property and life are (or at any rate, should be) protected by society, society is of advantage to him. There is in fact a mutual relationship of advantage to both (this idea of mutual benefit finds an echo in Letter LXXVI, § 3, and Letter CIV, § 1). If the citizen breaks the law, say by murdering, he is infringing the advantage of other citizens, and consequently deserves to forfeit some of his own advantage. The mutual relationship between one citizen and another, and between the citizen and society, can be seen both as a simple fact, and as a fact which gives rise to certain duties: it is thus a relationship implying what is appropriate, 'un rapport de convenance'. A similar analysis could be made of the relationship between parents and children, a relationship which, for Usbek, has important political consequences (CXXIX).

These examples may seem trite, but Montesquieu certainly would not have seen them in that way. An apparently more serious objection is that Usbek seems to be putting them forward as being universally valid, thus abandoning his relativism. If he had been challenged on this point, he might have replied that these are general laws of justice and morality, derived empirically from factors found in all societies, however different they may be in other respects.

[1] It is true that he throws doubt on this affirmation by adding: 'et, quand elle en dépendrait, ce serait une vérité terrible, qu'il faudrait se dérober à soi-même' (§ 7), but we can perhaps attribute this momentary hesitation to his dislike of dogmatism, rather than to uncertainty.

Having given his definition of justice, in Letter LXXXIII, Usbek continues by asking why, in spite of the existence of the *rapports de convenance*, men still act immorally. His answer is that '[ils] ne voient pas toujours ces rapports'—their reason is not sufficiently developed; and secondly that, even when they do see them, 'ils s'en éloignent', basically because of self-interest, and because their reason is clouded by their passions (§ 3). He then goes on to discuss the difference between men, who err for the reasons mentioned, and God, who always sees and follows justice, and he urges us to resemble God in this respect. This seems more like exhortation than argument, until we realize that when he talks of 'Dieu', Usbek is not referring to a personal God or to a Creator, still less to the God of any established religion, but simply to a hypothetical being who could be considered as the embodiment of the idea of perfect justice—an idea he believes we are all capable of having if we can overcome our passions and our prejudices through the use of our reason.

Having shown that man is potentially able to discover justice through his reason, and to put it into practice, without the help of religion, Usbek continues:

> Nous sommes entourés d'hommes plus forts que nous; ils peuvent nous nuire de mille manières différentes. . . . Quel repos pour nous de savoir qu'il y a dans le cœur de tous ces hommes un principe intérieur qui combat en notre faveur. . . ! (§ 8)

It might be thought that this 'principe' is an innate instinct of morality, a feeling which impels men to act virtuously, but there is no evidence, from the rest of the letter, that such is Usbek's meaning. The most he can be said to have shown about human instincts is that men are not naturally wicked (§ 4). The 'principe', then, is not an instinct: it is the awareness, in mankind, of the existence of the 'rapports' of morality, which must be respected if society is to exist and if individual happiness is to be ensured. An additional advantage of the act of respecting these 'rapports' is that it results, in the individual, in a feeling of satisfaction at having 'le cœur juste' (§ 11).

We have already been familiarized with these ideas earlier on in the *Lettres persanes*, in the fable of the Troglodytes (XI–XIV), which, like Letter LXXXIII, comes from the pen of Usbek. A friend has written to him to ask him to explain what he meant when he used to say that:

> les hommes étaient nés pour être vertueux, et que la justice est une qualité qui leur est aussi propre que l'existence. (X)

We notice that Usbek is not reported as saying that 'les hommes étaient nés vertueux', but that they are 'nes *pour être* vertueux', that is, that their nature is such that they can survive only by being virtuous. The fable itself illustrates precisely this: Usbek imagines a degenerate tribe of violent and selfish people, the Troglodytes; tired of the constraints of law, they assassinated their rulers, and each person decided to look after his own interests, 'sans consulter ceux des autres' (XI, § 6). Usbek gives a series of examples of how this selfishness always resulted in a loss rather than a gain to the individual who practised it (§§ 8–14); the wicked Troglodytes soon perished 'par leur méchanceté même' (XII, § 1).

However, there survived two men who had not practised the selfishness of their compatriots, but who 'aimaient la vertu', partly because such was their character ('ils avaient de l'humanité'), but also because 'ils connaissaient la justice' (XII, § 1), that is, their reason told them that 'l'intérêt des particuliers se trouve toujours dans l'intérêt commun' (XII, § 2); they learned from experience that generosity and humanity towards others tend to ensure their love and co-operation, and hence individual and communal happiness. Far from believing in innate virtue, they saw that it was vitally necessary, in order to prevent a recurrence of the evils which had characterized the wicked Troglodytes, constantly to remind their children of that terrible example, and to educate them 'à la vertu' (XII, § 2).[2] This acquired virtue is the source of their happiness and prosperity, which is, paradoxically, threatened as the community expands (XIV).

It could be said that the fable puts forward a facile view of virtue, and this is true in a sense ('la vertu n'est point une chose qui doive nous coûter' is one of the Troglodyte maxims—XII, § 2), in that once acquired, it gives pleasure; but it is not true insofar as constant effort is needed to acquire it and to pass it on to the next generation. The fable of the Troglodytes does not prove that man is naturally just, but that he must practise justice if he is to survive in society. In the *Lettres persanes*, morality emerges as a rational, not an instinctive, force.[3]

---

[2] Montesquieu stresses this point in the unpublished continuation of the fable, where a Troglodyte says to the second king: 'Vous connaissez, Seigneur, la base sur quoi est fondée la vertu de votre peuple: c'est sur l'éducation' (Garnier edition, p. 337).

[3] It is true that Usbek talks of a natural instinct of virtue or modesty in women (XXVI), but in the light of the constraints he has to exercise on his wives and of their final revolt, as well as of the behaviour of European women as seen through the eyes of Rica, we have the impression that he is deceiving himself.

The principles of Montesquieu's philosophy, which is aimed at producing self-knowledge, tolerance and justice, can be summarized as follows: most men are not naturally virtuous, but they are capable of becoming virtuous through the use of their reason; they must be made aware of the often irrational nature of their acts and of the generally subjective nature of their judgements; they must learn to view the world more objectively, so as to establish criteria of justice and morality valid for their own society; these criteria can be valid for other societies only if the same needs and conditions are found there too. Montesquieu's philosophy is socially oriented, and this is nowhere more apparent than in his thinking about religion.

(ii) Institutions: religion

In reading the Lettres persanes, it is important to be aware of the differences between the way religion was conceived and practised in eighteenth-century France, and what it means today. Nowadays, especially in Protestant countries, Christianity is often understood as a belief in the brotherhood of men, in the desirability of improving their lot on earth, in God as a benevolent father and creator, and possibly in Christ, but as an example, rather than as a saviour. This conception of religion is very similar to the idea of deism, which became popular in the eighteenth century through the writings of philosophers such as Voltaire and Rousseau: the deist claims to reject all dogma, but believes in a God who is concerned with the morality of human actions. For the Church, deism was as bad as atheism, since the orthodox view was that human nature has been totally corrupt since the Fall, that we can only be saved through the intercession of Christ, and that our life on earth should be devoted primarily, if not exclusively, to achieving that salvation.

The second difference is that whereas now divergencies of opinion on matters of faith are usually accepted as normal, in the seventeenth and eighteenth centuries they often resulted in religious persecution. The Catholic Church, in particular, was intent on crushing heresy with the help of the secular powers.

The third difference concerns the sincerity of religious belief. Today, those who claim to be religious are on the whole sincere, because there are relatively few material advantages to be gained from belief; in the seventeenth and eighteenth centuries, the case was different, and hypocrisy was more widespread. It took two forms: there was the hypocrisy of the unorthodox person, anxious to avoid persecution; it consisted in falsely naïve expressions of orthodoxy and respect for religion, such as we find in Montesquieu's 'Réflexions', where, referring to himself by the pronoun 'on', he attempts to exonerate himself from Gaultier's censures:

> Bien loin qu'on pensât à intéresser [understand 'critiquer'] quelque principe de notre religion, on ne soupçonnait pas même d'imprudence. (§ 6)

Then there was the hypocrisy found among the clergy. For those at the top of the ecclesiastical hierarchy, religion was often a lucrative profession rather than a vocation; hence the large number of *abbés commendataires*: such *abbés* were usually noblemen who had received the tonsure in order to be able to draw an income from an abbey of which they were appointed the nominal head, but where they rarely resided; they often lived very worldly lives—in Letter XXVIII, there is an example of one who has seduced a *danseuse* at the *Opéra*.

It is against this background that Montesquieu's religious criticism in the *Lettres persanes* should be viewed. The criticism concerns two main features of religious life: firstly, dogma, and secondly, what may be called the theological mentality and its effects, that is, the attitudes towards life and society to be found among theologians, the clergy, and believers in general, together with the social results of those attitudes.

Many of the dogmas at that time essential to Christianity are attacked, either directly or through the use of irony, by Montesquieu's Persians, whom he blithely exonerates from blame by claiming that, as foreigners, they are ignorant of the profound justifications for those dogmas ('Réflexions', § 6).

In Letter CXIII, Usbek throws doubt on the Creation, at least in the biblical version, by alluding to the view of certain 'philosophes' that for God to have made the universe at a certain point in time would imply a lack of consistency on His part, which would be incompatible with the perfection of His nature. That basic tenet of Christianity, the Fall of man, is not so much criticized as merely discarded by Usbek: it runs counter to his belief, expressed in Letter LXXXIII, that man is not naturally wicked, and that he can achieve virtue through his own efforts, by exercising and heeding his reason. Usbek makes no mention here of grace or redemption: for him, they are quite irrelevant to social morality. If there is an afterlife, it can be obtained by all, regardless of creed—such, at least, is the implication of Letter XXXV, in spite of its ostensible suggestion that all men are Moslems at heart.

The theologians who try to impose such dogmas on others are shown to be incapable of justifying them rationally: Méhémet-Hali's reply to Usbek's questions about religious notions of impurity (XVIII) illustrates this fact.

Such irrationality would not matter if it had no influence on social life, but unfortunately, so Montesquieu suggests through his characters, it does. The leaders of the Church, realizing that their precepts are not practicable in society, readily grant dispensations. As Rica ironically puts it:

comme on a jugé qu'il est moins aisé de remplir ses devoirs que d'avoir des évêques qui en dispensent, on a pris ce dernier parti pour l'utilité publique. (XXIX)

—the implication being that it would be better not to make the laws in the first place, since to dispense people from obedience (especially when they can buy such dispensation) is to throw discredit on all law, good and bad. An example of this kind of corrupting effect is to be found in the letter about the casuist, who sees his job as enabling Christians to get to heaven 'à meilleur marché qu'il est possible', that is, with the least possible moral effort, by informing them how much evil they can get away with before they are actually damned (LVII). Usbek's indignation towards the casuist is not caused by any belief that all religious laws should be observed to the letter, but by his conviction that there should be a small number of laws, all directed solely towards the good of society, and all strictly observed (XLVI, § 2).

It is not only individual conduct that is threatened by the theological mentality: collective security is also endangered, when a group of individuals, motivated by religion, take it upon themselves to promote their particular point of view by threats or violence. It was Montesquieu's opinion (as it was Voltaire's) that 'en matière de Religion, plus le sujet de la dispute est léger, plus elle devient violente';[4] in saying this, Montesquieu is suggesting that those who can prove their views rationally have no need to resort to violence, whereas those who cannot have to rely on coercion to try to convince others. This theme is the subject of part of Letter XXIX, where Rica shows that theological disputes lead to public disorder. This had certainly been the case in France

[4] Fragment of the *Lettres persanes* (Garnier edition, p. 347).

in the second half of the sixteenth century, with the wars of religion between Catholics and Huguenots. Rica underlines the irony of the situation by saying 'il n'y a jamais eu de royaume où il y ait eu tant de guerres civiles que dans celui du Christ.' In Montesquieu's time, there was perhaps not so much physical violence in the name of religion, but the interminable disputes between Jansenists and Jesuits constituted an equally pernicious threat to public order; here the condemnation is expressed by a priest who describes to Usbek some of the difficulties of his calling: 'nous troublons l'État, nous nous tourmentons nous-mêmes pour faire recevoir des points de religion qui ne sont point fondamentaux' (LXI).

Theologians, and those who put their ideas into practice, namely the clergy, are thus shown to be responsible for causing much social upheaval, and worse still, as a result of the spirit of proselytism which prompts Christians to attempt the conversion of the whole world, this malady is spread to other, previously peaceable parts of the globe. Rica has no good to say of such missionary activities (XLIX). To try to force others to accept certain beliefs is, as Usbek shows, both inhuman and psychologically impracticable (LXXXV, last paragraph).

Even more reprehensible, in Montesquieu's view, is the way in which the Church interferes in a domain which properly belongs to the state, namely the punishment of crime, by putting to death or imprisoning those supposedly guilty of offences against religion. In Letter XXIX Rica, adopting a falsely naïve attitude, mocks one of the worst examples of such interference, the Inquisition in Spain and Portugal (§ 6); his mockery turns to indignation, as he shows how the courts of the Inquisition do not even respect the normal fair procedures which should characterize the administration of justice (§ 7).

There was no Inquisition in France, but similar though less extreme kinds of interference were common, the most notorious being the French government's decision to make Protestantism illegal by revoking the Edict of Nantes (1685). This decision, prompted by the *dévots*, inflicted damage on the French economy and on French prestige, since the many Protestants who chose the illegal[5] course of exiling themselves, rather than being converted, took with them their skills and their resentment. Letter LXXXV stresses, through an allegory, the economic damage caused by the revocation.

[5] Illegal, that is, for laymen. Protestant ministers who refused to be converted were legally obliged to go into exile.

More subtly pernicious, in Montesquieu's opinion, was the way in which the Church induced the state to introduce laws and institutions which, having a purely religious aim, were irrelevant or even contrary to the aims of society. The examples he gives, through Usbek, are those of the laws encouraging celibacy and monastic institutions, which, so he claims, in common with many eighteenth-century thinkers, were responsible for a decline in the population (CXVII), and the law forbidding divorce, which had the same effect (CXVI). Usbek even goes so far as to suggest that the law against suicide, being religious in origin, and having no value to society, should be abolished (LXXVI), a view which Montesquieu later either abandoned, or felt it prudent to contradict, for, when he came to revise the *Lettres persanes* shortly before his death, he inserted an extra letter (LXXVII), arguing the opposite point of view.

In spite of these evils resulting from the theological mentality, Montesquieu nowhere suggests that religion itself should be abolished (in fact, comparatively few of his contemporaries advocated atheism, even in private). On the contrary, he argued that, rightly interpreted, it could be of considerable value to society. This view is put forward in Letters XLVI and LXXXV, both written by Usbek.

In Letter LXXXV he proposes a remedy for socially undesirable manifestations of 'la dévotion' (such as the revocation of the Edict of Nantes); as often happens, he expresses tentatively an idea of which he is quite firmly convinced:

> Je ne sais pas . . . s'il n'est pas bon que dans un état il y ait plusieurs religions.

In justification of this proposal, he claims that members of sects other than the official one tend to be more useful to society because, deprived by their beliefs of access to a career in the government, they apply their energies to activities which, though scorned by public opinion (Montesquieu is thinking of commerce), are essential to the prosperity of a country. In addition, since all religious sects 'contiennent des préceptes utiles à la Société' (that is, since they all stress the punishment of crime and the reward of virtue, in an afterlife or on earth), consequently, 'il est bon qu'elles soient observées avec zèle.' 'Or,' he concludes, 'qu'y a-t-il de plus capable d'animer ce zèle que leur multiplicité?' He goes on to argue that such zealous moral rivalry will not produce public disturbance unless one of the sects becomes dominant and tries to abolish the others. Usbek's proposal, which is in some ways fairly similar to the actual situation prevailing in England at the time, offers an ingenious and realistic solution to the problem of channelling religious zeal in socially useful directions. However, it is a solution which, in Montesquieu's eyes, is only a second best.

The ideal solution, as expressed through Usbek in Letter XLVI, would be one which ensured that religion is completely shorn of its potentially dangerous irrational and sectarian elements, and where belief in God would result above all in acts of social morality and in love of one's fellow-citizens. Although he does not use the word, Usbek is here proposing the doctrine of deism.

His reasoning is that although all men agree that 'le premier objet d'un homme religieux [est] de plaire à la Divinité', most religious people, having the mistaken assumption that certain ceremonies are what please God, waste their time arguing about which are the correct ones; whereas in Usbek's opinion it is obvious that the 'moyen le plus sûr' of pleasing God is 'd'observer les règles de la société et les devoirs de l'humanité.' Here, as in Letter LXXXIII, God becomes more or less a synonym of human justice.

Montesquieu's conception of religion is utilitarian: religion is valid insofar as it is an aid to social cohesion; its spiritual side is best eliminated, since it is subjective and potentially divisive. Nowhere does he admit that it is right for people to have spiritual needs which can be fulfilled only by communion with a deity.[6] This utilitarian approach to religion, and this hostility towards its spiritual and institutional aspects, are the reflection of Montesquieu's positive thinking about the nature of man as a social being. The changes he is suggesting in religion are part of his more general view of the nature and purpose of society.

(iii) Institutions: politics

Many political writers of the seventeenth and eighteenth centuries felt obliged to explain how society came into existence. They usually imagined a pre-social state of mankind (called the *state of nature*), and described its development first into a social state, then into a political state.

---

[6] Montesquieu did not include in the *Lettres persanes* a letter he had drafted, in which Usbek, on his journey to Europe, appears to exhibit strong religious feelings (Garnier edition, pp. 353–4).

Their purpose was not so preposterous as it might appear to those who believe that man has always been a social being. They were aiming to establish a basis for moral behaviour and a basis for sovereignty (in this context, the right of exercising political power). For them, pre-social man is to be understood as 'man-without-laws'; they were trying to determine how such a man would behave towards others when he came into contact with them, and consequently what sort of constraints might have to be imposed to make social existence possible. The implication behind such questions is, how just are the laws of the societies we now live in?

If man-without-laws is a savage creature, as the English philosopher Hobbes thought, then he will need strong laws and an authoritarian government in order to live in society (Hobbes was, to a certain extent, trying to justify the monarchy of the Stuarts). If, on the other hand, man-without-laws is basically a peaceable fellow, with a desire to secure his own safety and comfort, but with little desire to hurt others, and a strong realization that to do so would place his own safety in jeopardy, then he will need a moderate government, which will protect his rights to his own property, and leave him much freedom. This is what another English philosopher, Locke, suggested (he was partly justifying the revolution of 1689, which dethroned the Stuarts and instituted a more constitutional monarchy).

Montesquieu was very interested in the kind of questions which Hobbes and Locke were asking, about the nature of man and of political power, but he did not set about answering them in quite the same way. Indeed, he makes Usbek mock the philosophers who seek the origin of society:

> Je n'ai jamais ouï parler du droit public qu'on n'ait commencé par rechercher soigneusement quelle est l'origine des sociétés, ce qui me paraît ridicule. Si les hommes n'en formaient point, s'ils se quittaient et se fuyaient les uns les autres, il faudrait en demander la raison. . . . Mais ils naissent tous liés les uns aux autres; un fils est né auprès de son père, et il s'y tient: voilà la société et la cause de la société. (XCIV)

Here, Usbek is evidently unaware of the political purpose behind the theory he scorns; but in fact he himself, in examining the question of sovereignty, comes close to admitting that political society (though not informal society, based on the family) came into existence through a kind of agreement which subsequently affected the way in which political power is exercised and accepted.

In Letter CIV, he gives an account of the view of certain English political writers about 'la soumission et l'obéissance' owed by subjects to their rulers:

> Selon eux, il n'y a qu'un lien qui puisse attacher les hommes, qui est celui de la gratitude: un mari, une femme, un père et un fils ne sont liés entre eux que par l'amour qu'ils se portent, ou par les bienfaits qu'ils se procurent, et ces motifs divers de reconnaissance sont l'origine de tous les royaumes et de toutes les sociétés. (§ 1)

This looks like a further example of a 'rapport de convenance' (though Usbek does not use the expression here). Informal society, namely the family, consists of a group of people united for mutual advantage; this is the 'factual' aspect of the relationship; from it Usbek derives the duty, which falls upon political leaders, to ensure that formal or political society should result in the same advantage for all. Hence, 'tout pouvoir sans bornes ne saurait être légitime', so, if 'un prince, bien loin de faire vivre ses sujets heureux, veut les accabler et les détruire', the latter may consider themselves free, in other words they may depose him. Usbek tries to conceal his sympathy for these libertarian views about the origin of society and the consequent nature of political power, by prefacing Letter CIV with the comment that they are 'bien extraordinaires', a phrase which we may interpret as meaning that although those accustomed to absolutism might find them extraordinary, they are reasonable.

The other place where Usbek examines the origin of society and of political power is the story of the Troglodytes. The new race of virtuous Troglodytes is descended from two families (XII); this is in accordance with the theory of Letter CIV; their paternalistic government proved to be no longer suitable when the population increased, so the Troglodytes 'crurent qu'il était à propos de se choisir un roi'; by mutual agreement, they decided 'qu'il fallait déférer la couronne à celui qui était le plus juste'; the chosen man, 'un vieillard vénérable', accepted the charge, though with the greatest reluctance (XIV). Montesquieu wrote a continuation to the story, which he did not publish: in it, the king died of grief at the passing of the old order, with its emphasis on virtue; a new king was elected, 'le plus sage et le plus juste', from among the former king's family.[7] This strange mixture of an elective and a hereditary monarchy is again comparable to the society based on gratitude outlined in Letter

[7] Garnier edition, pp. 336–7.

CIV. The whole story shows that, for Usbek, informal society has no artificial beginning, but that political society does, and indeed must have if justice is to be safeguarded.

The safeguarding of justice is, in Usbek's view, only one of the functions of political society. The other main function is the safeguarding of liberty. Liberty, in the political sense, here means the absence of constraints on the citizen except insofar as they are strictly necessary to public order. The absence of unnecessary constraints is the principle behind Usbek's thinking in Letter LXXX, where he defines 'le gouvernement le plus conforme à la raison' as:

> celui qui va à son but à moins de frais; de sorte que celui qui conduit les hommes de la manière qui convient le plus à leur penchant et à leur inclination est le plus parfait.
>
> Si, dans un gouvernement doux, le peuple est aussi soumis que dans un gouvernement sévère, le premier est préférable, puisqu'il est plus conforme à la raison, et que la séverité est un motif étranger.

When Usbek says here that people should be governed 'de la manière qui convient le plus à leur penchant et à leur inclination', he is not advocating the system we apparently have today, where governments often claim to be influenced by public opinion; it is not the opinion of the citizens that is important here, but their characteristics, which will affect the degree of severity necessary to ensure public order. Although Usbek's argument here is fundamentally inspired by humanitarianism, he presents it in a relativistic manner, and his condemnation of excessive severity is based on practical considerations: severe punishments are ineffective, in that they tend to blur the distinction between petty and serious crime, and to accustom men to violence (LXXX, § 5), and since, on a political level, excessive constraint causes people to revolt against the government (LXXX, §§ 6–13, and CII).

Public order, for Montesquieu, is not an aim to be sought for its own sake, merely a prerequisite to liberty. Nor does he consider that the kind of tranquillity known as 'national unity' is very important, except for small communities such as that of the Troglodytes, whose success depended on the fact that they saw themselves as 'une seule famille' (XII). In larger states, political conflict can be a sign of liberty: in the works of the historians of England, 'on voit la liberté sortir sans cesse des feux de la discorde et de la sédition: le Prince toujours chancelant sur un trône inébranlable' (CXXXVI).

Another aspect of the political life of the English admired by Montesquieu is the fact that they encourage commerce (same letter), and it is clear, from the *Lettres persanes*, that he believes that besides justice and liberty, nations should have more tangible aims, namely, wealth and populousness.

By wealth, Montesquieu does not understand the possession of money. This is apparent from the letters concerned with the Law crisis, and especially from Letter CXLVI, where Usbek is pretending to talk about 'les Indes', but is in fact alluding to the France of the Regency:

> J'ai vu la foi des contrats bannie, les plus saintes conventions anéanties, toutes les lois des familles renversées. . . .
>
> J'ai vu naître soudain, dans tous les cœurs, une soif insatiable de richesses. J'ai vu se former en un moment une détestable conjuration de s'enrichir, non par un honnête travail et une généreuse industrie, mais par la ruine du prince, de l'État et des concitoyens.

It is clear from this that Usbek is not opposed to the acquisition of wealth 'par un honnête travail', only to speculation. In fact he sees national wealth as a source of political strength: Letter CVI shows him arguing that it is essential for kings to encourage 'les arts' (by which is to be understood craft and manufacture), in order for their countries to be strong enough to defend themselves against foreign invasion. Usbek is opposed to the retention of capital by a small number of individuals, particularly if they are the clergy, and believes that the development of commerce and industry is dependent on the rapid circulation of money among the largest number of people:

> Les dervis ont en leurs mains presque toutes les richesses de l'État;. . . Tant de richesses tombent, pour ainsi dire, en paralysie: plus de circulation, plus de commerce, plus d'arts, plus de manufactures. (CXVII)

He praises the Romans for encouraging individual effort in commerce (CXV).

National wealth is linked with the size of a country's population; wealth and populousness are a sign of prosperity:

> Plus il y a d'hommes dans un état, plus le commerce y fleurit; . . . plus le commerce y fleurit, plus le nombre des hommes y augmente: ces deux choses s'entraident et se favorisent nécessairement. (CXV)

In addition, both population and wealth are affected by the degree of liberty within a state: the Turkish empire has a declining population, little commerce, and no political freedom (XIX); the three factors are interrelated.

The principles of justice, liberty, national wealth and populousness provide pointers to Montesquieu's assessment of the relative value of different political institutions. For reasons which will soon become obvious, he concentrates most of his attention on monarchy, and on what he considers to be its degenerate form, despotism. He chooses Usbek, an aristocrat exiled because of a despotic regime, for his main spokesman.

Usbek does not apparently view the political regimes of the continent of his exile with much optimism:

> La plupart des gouvernements d'Europe sont monarchiques, ou plutôt sont ainsi appelés: car je ne sais pas s'il y en a jamais eu véritablement de tels. . . . C'est un état violent, qui dégénère toujours en despotisme ou en république: la puissance ne peut jamais être également partagée entre le peuple et le prince; l'équilibre est trop difficile à garder. (CII)

However, Usbek continues by showing that although European monarchs have, in theory, absolute power, they do not exercise it, because they have to respect 'les mœurs et la religion des peuples' and because they do not wish to arouse opposition and thereby weaken their position, which, as Usbek goes on to say, is exactly the effect of the exercising of absolute power by the Persian rulers. Thus, though Usbek shows that European monarchies are in danger of becoming despotic, he admits that at present they more or less succeed in preserving a balance between the King and the people, however precarious that balance may be. When he says that monarchy is 'un état violent qui dégénère', he is presumably calling attention to the difficulty of maintaining it in its purity, rather than condemning it.

For Usbek, the essential characteristic of monarchy is that political power should somehow be shared between the king and the people. What does this mean? Letter CXXXI, written by the thoughtful Rhédi, on the subject of the history of the monarchical form of government, provides an explanation: the nordic tribes which invaded Europe and put an end to the Roman Empire (which Rhédi sees as a despotic government), were free, because 'ils bornaient si fort l'autorité de leurs rois qu'ils n'étaient proprement que des chefs ou des généraux'; he

instances tribes where the king could be deposed as soon as the subjects
became dissatisfied with him, or where the 'seigneurs' shared political
power with him. This letter is echoed by Letter CXXXVI, where those
same nordic tribes are said to have enjoyed 'cette douce liberté, si
conforme à la raison, à l'humanité et à la nature'; the three terms used here
are not synonymous: 'raison' refers to what is sensible and practicable,
'humanité' to feelings of compassion or fairness, and 'nature' to the rights
which every human being should enjoy by the mere fact of his existence.
Montesquieu, in this formula, is suggesting that it is both foolish and
morally wrong to curtail unnecessarily the liberty of the subject.

The French nobility is shown still to enjoy some liberty, in that the
king does not dare to put a noble to death if the latter has offended him
(CII); the French king is even said, by a Frenchman whose words are
reported by Usbek, to be 'jaloux de l'honneur du dernier de ses sujets'
(LXXXIX).

Another limit imposed on French monarchs was the privileges
accorded to the *Parlements*: they traditionally had the right of registering,
and even of commenting on, new laws introduced by the king.
However, as Usbek observes, it was the policy of Louis XIV to reduce
their privileges: 'ces grands corps . . . ont cédé . . . à l'autorité suprême, qui
a tout abattu' (XCII); and quite early during his stay in France, he had
slyly alluded to the despotic tendencies of the great monarch:

> On dit que [Louis XIV] possède à un très haut degré le talent de se faire
> obéir: il gouverne avec le même génie sa famille, sa cour, son état. On
> lui a souvent entendu dire que, de tous les gouvernements du Monde,
> celui des Turcs ou celui de notre auguste sultan lui plairait le mieux,
> tant il fait cas de la politique orientale. (XXXVII)

The warning could hardly have been sounded more clearly.

It has long been obvious to historians that Montesquieu's picture of
Persia and Turkey as afflicted by arbitrary and despotic regimes is, to say
the least, an exaggeration. But he was less concerned with historical
accuracy, in the *Lettres persanes*, than with teaching his compatriots an
indirect lesson in the disadvantages of political absolutism and the
advantages of moderate government.

According to Usbek, the despotic government is characterized by the
'immense pouvoir' or 'autorité illimitée' exercised by the king over his
subjects, particularly in the punishment of supposed crimes against the
state, which are treated with the utmost severity: this harshness tends to

have the effect of encouraging rather than preventing revolution (CII); the despot can obtain the co-operation of his subjects only by intimidating them (LXXXIX), and he tends, out of fear, to hide himself away from them. Consequently, they do not care if he is deposed (CIII): despotism is thus an inefficient form of government, since it makes no attempt to tap the potential loyalty of the subject. These criticisms relate to the principle established in Letter LXXX, namely that moderation is the essential characteristic of a good government.

Montesquieu's interest in political theory is by no means confined to the question of the distribution and exercise of power. Any political and social matter relevant to liberty and prosperity comes within his domain, in this work of extensive implications.

Montesquieu shows great interest in the subject of the law. In some ways, his position is quite conservative. In Letter CXXIX, although Usbek begins by pointing to the inadequacy of the legislation of many countries (irrational or prejudiced attitudes on the part of legislators, their concern for 'des détails inutiles', their use of Latin instead of the mother tongue), even so, 'quelles que soient les lois, il faut toujours les suivre': the implication is that if they are not respected, with all their imperfections, the administration of justice will become arbitrary, and arbitrariness is worse than injustice, because it has no measure. If laws are to be changed, as is sometimes necessary, then this must be done with great formality, for otherwise people will conclude that the law is not very important. These views are not fashionable today, but there is a certain psychological validity in what Usbek is saying. Similar psychological realism is to be found in his views about the punishment of crime, which happen to be more in accordance with present-day beliefs: he condemns the lack of proportion, frequently found in eighteenth-century penal law, between the crime committed and the punishment inflicted, and he shows that it is misguided to suppose that harsh penalties will automatically produce a reduction in the number of offences (LXXX).

Montesquieu's condemnation of harsh penalties is not primarily based on emotional principles, but on his assessment of how human beings behave: he is above all concerned with the appropriateness of legislation, that is, with the relationship between the needs of society on the one hand, and the legal and administrative system required to satisfy those needs, on the other. This aspect of the *Lettres persanes*, which is often called the 'sociological aspect', is apparent as early as the story of the Troglodytes –

Letter XIV shows that a patriarchal system of government is no longer suitable for an expanding population—but it is mainly found in Letters CXIII–CXXII; it gives the work a very modern look, and counteracts the conservatism found in other letters.

Admittedly, the problem with which Letters CXIII–CXXII are concerned is a false one: Ubsek is trying to discover why the population of the world is decreasing, when in fact throughout the eighteenth century, it was on the increase (that of France rose from about 18 million to about 25 million during the century, though this was a development of which thinkers at the time, including Montesquieu, were largely unaware). However, the method applied by Usbek is still basically valid.

In the first five letters of the series, he is dealing with causes which influence the size of the population of Europe. In Letter CXIII, he isolates what may be called a 'physical' cause, namely diseases old and new; Letters CXIV–CXVII are concerned with 'mental' causes, that is, attitudes of mind, fostered by certain religions or institutions. Since the decline of the Roman Empire, where legislation and custom encouraged the growth of the population (CXV), the two dominant religions, Moslem and Christian, have caused the population to decline, the former because it favours polygamy (CXIV), the latter by its refusal to allow divorce, thus perpetuating infertile marriages (CXVI), and by its idealization of celibacy, especially in Catholic countries (CXVII). The remaining letters of the series deal with the populousness of other parts of the world, which is shown to be influenced negatively by factors such as slavery (CXVIII) and colonization (CXXI), or the way of life of certain tribes (CXX), and positively by certain religious beliefs (non-Christian, of course) (CXIX), as well as by 'la douceur du gouvernement', that is, by political freedom (CXXII).

These letters, although they constitute, by their total length and their unity of subject, a break with the normally diverse intellectual structure of the *Lettres persanes*, are perfectly in accordance with one of the main aims of the work, namely the improvement of social existence and the development of political liberty, having regard to the specific conditions prevailing in each country. They are quite remarkable for their analytic approach and for their utilization of a wide variety of historical and political facts (sometimes dubious ones) to establish a particular theory. Besides being an examination of political phenomena, they also propose reforms in certain domains (especially that of the relation between the Church and the state), with a view to bringing about desirable political aims.

Montesquieu's wish to see political change in certain areas is also exemplified in his thought on international law, which he calls 'le droit public', and which he discusses in Letters XCIV and XCV. For Usbek, who writes these letters, 'le droit public' should be thought of as 'un droit civil . . . du monde', that is, it should be administered as impartially as civil law within any country; instead of this, it has been corrupted into 'une science qui apprend aux princes jusqu'à quel point ils peuvent violer la justice sans choquer leurs intérêts'—perhaps he is alluding to the dubious territorial claims made by Louis XIV over parts of Europe which he wished to incorporate into the French kingdom. Montesquieu has a fairly optimistic view of the possibility of eradicating this attitude to international law: 'les sujets de disputes sont presque toujours clairs et faciles à terminer. . . . Il ne faut qu'aimer la justice pour la trouver'. This naïve optimism is echoed in Letter CVI, where Usbek tries to persuade Rhédi that if some immensely powerful weapon were invented, it would soon be prohibited by international agreement.

In Letter XCV, Usbek sets out what he sees as the principles which should govern international justice: war is justified when a country has to defend itself, or an ally, against invasion. He is thus no pacifist, but he does suggest alternatives to war, such as non-belligerent reprisals, and the ending of alliances. In Letter CXXI, he condemns a major cause of international conflict, colonization; the condemnation is mainly based on practical and humanitarian considerations, as is his indictment of slavery (CXVIII, CXXI).

Montesquieu's outlook is universalist, in the sense that he wishes to show, not that one country is immensely superior to another, but that all have something of value to offer to the world, either by their prosperity, or by their political system, or by their culture. The words which he attributes to Usbek's friend Ibben characterize this attitude:

En quelque pays que j'aie été, j'y ai vécu comme si j'avais dû y passer ma vie. (LXVII)

5. Conclusion

Although the *Lettres persanes* aim at depicting France, with its virtues, its defects and its oddities, they also, more profoundly, attempt to place the characteristics of a particular nation in a wider perspective, and to make the reader aware of the conditional and ephemeral nature of what he might tend to see as permanent and universal; they do this by unmasking prejudice, and by showing what lessons may be learned from the example of other nations. The work suggests goals—greater political and religious liberty, greater emphasis on national rather than individual wealth—and a method of preliminary investigation prior to achieving them, through a careful study of the multiple factors which must be taken into account when any kind of social or political change is envisaged. In the light of these far-reaching aims, the slight traces of reactionary attitudes, and the occasional tendency to oversimplify, melt into comparative insignificance.

The form of the *Lettres persanes*, so perplexing at first sight, reflects Montesquieu's desire for reassessment. Merely to tell somebody they have prejudices is to prompt him to find reasons to justify them, and to return the compliment too. To begin, as Montesquieu does, by not making one's own standpoint too obvious, by questioning all attitudes in turn, and to work towards a clarification of problems and a tentative proposal of solutions to them, constitutes an invitation to fruitful reflection which it is hard to ignore. Montesquieu is not interested in quick results in the form of new but perhaps equally harmful prejudices or institutions. He is the very opposite of a propagandist; rather, he is a thinker who wishes to encourage a rationalistic attitude among those prepared to listen to him.

The spirit of rationalism is the predominant intellectual feature of the *Lettres persanes*, and, as such, it satisfies our desire for unity of thought; but what makes the work so pleasing to read is above all its diversity. It introduces us to the sensuous and often bloody world of the orient, with its despots and its harems; and to the sophisticated salons, and even the dingy garrets, of eighteenth-century Paris. There are discussions about all manner of topics, from the nature of justice and religion to the size of women's coiffures, from the origin of society to facetious methods of curing insomnia. The language is as varied as the subject-matter, being, in turn, candid, ironic, witty, tragic, indignant, erotic, figurative or direct. Behind all these facets, we glimpse an ideal of order which explains human life without reducing it to uniformity. The ideal is often hidden from us by the richness of the images, hidden partly because we do not like to be presented with a naked truth, and partly because, in the early eighteenth century, one had to be circumspect if one talked about 'les grands sujets'. Yet the veil with which Montesquieu conceals his purpose is as pleasing as his ideas are challenging.

Suggestions for Further Reading

Several satisfactory paperback editions of the *Lettres persanes* are available, the best being that prepared by J. Starobinski (Paris, Gallimard, 1973), but they mostly lack explanatory notes.

The best annotated edition is the one by P. Vernière (Paris, Classiques Garnier, 1960; revised edition 1975); the edition by A. Adam (Paris and Geneva, Droz, 1954), is also good.

Readers seeking accurate and up-to-date information about Montesquieu, and an authoritative critical assessment of his works, including the *Lettres persanes*, should consult R. Shackleton, *Montesquieu, A Critical Biography* (Oxford University Press, 1961). Two older and shorter studies are still of considerable value: A. Sorel, *Montesquieu* (Paris, Hachette, 1887 and later reprints), and J. Dedieu, *Montesquieu, l'homme et l'œuvre* (Paris, Boivin, 1943, reprinted, under the title *Montesquieu*, Paris, Hatier, 1966).

V. Mylne, *The Eighteenth-Century French Novel* (Manchester University Press, 1965, pp. 144–55), and J. Rousset, *Forme et Signification* (Paris, Corti, 1962, pp. 65–108), both have excellent chapters on the novel in letter form.

There are many useful short articles on the *Lettres persanes*. Four of the most interesting are:

R. Grimsley, 'The idea of nature in Montesquieu's *Lettres persanes*', *French Studies* (1951), pp. 293–306. (A helpful analysis of the philosophical content of the work.)

R. Laufer, 'La réussite romanesque et la signification des *Lettres persanes* de Montesquieu', *Revue d'histoire littéraire de la France* (1961), pp. 188–203. (Laufer sees the fictional element as essential to the work, and regards Usbek as a tragic hero.)

R. Mercier, 'Le roman dans les *Lettres persanes*: structure et signification', *Revue des sciences humaines* (1962), pp. 345–56. (Mercier claims that the fictional element is subordinate to the philosophical element.)

R. Shackleton, 'The Moslem chronology of the *Lettres persanes*', *French Studies* (1954), pp. 17–27. (Shackleton solves the mystery of the dating of the letters.)